# GEORGE
# WASHINGTON
*and the*
# ART OF
# BUSINESS

# GEORGE WASHINGTON
# and the
# ART OF
# BUSINESS

## LEADERSHIP PRINCIPLES
## OF AMERICA'S FIRST
## COMMANDER-IN-CHIEF

*Mark McNeilly*

OXFORD
UNIVERSITY PRESS
2008

# OXFORD
UNIVERSITY PRESS

Oxford University Press, Inc., publishes works that further
Oxford University's objective of excellence
in research, scholarship, and education.

Oxford   New York
Auckland   Cape Town   Dar es Salaam   Hong Kong   Karachi
Kuala Lumpur   Madrid   Melbourne   Mexico City   Nairobi
New Delhi   Shanghai   Taipei   Toronto

With offices in
Argentina   Austria   Brazil   Chile   Czech Republic   France   Greece
Guatemala   Hungary   Italy   Japan   Poland   Portugal   Singapore
South Korea   Switzerland   Thailand   Turkey   Ukraine   Vietnam

Copyright © 2008 by Mark McNeilly

Published by Oxford University Press, Inc.
198 Madison Avenue, New York, NY 10016

www.oup.com

Oxford is a registered trademark of Oxford University Press

Library of Congress Cataloging-in-Publication Data
McNeilly, Mark.
George Washington and the art of business : leadership principles of
America's first commander-in-chief / by Mark McNeilly.
p. cm.
Includes bibliographical references and index.
ISBN 978-0-19-518978-0
1. Leadership. 2. Washington, George, 1732—1799. I. Title.
II. Title: Leadership principles of America's first commander-in-chief.
HM1261.M398 2007
658.4'092—dc22
2007018611

1   3   5   7   9   8   6   4   2

Printed in the United States of America
on acid-free paper

## HISTORICAL DEDICATION

*In honor of George Washington,*
*Warrior, Leader, Founding Father, Statesman,*
*Who gave so much of himself,*
*And to whom so much is owed.*


## PERSONAL DEDICATION

*To my parents, James and Esperanza, for their love,*
*To my wife, Sandy, for her help and support in all things,*
*To my children, Alex, Logan, and Kenzie, for sweetening my life,*
*And to God, who makes all things possible.*

# CONTENTS

# ACKNOWLEDGMENTS

I would like to express my appreciation to my editor, Herb Addison, for working with me on this book. His suggestions on the overall direction, organization, and examples were all important in making it better. Thanks are also due Dr. Steven Kreis, instructor of European history at American Public University, for reviewing the near-final manuscript to check historical accuracy. I also want to say thank you to my wife, Sandy, and my kids. Their patience with me during the two years spent writing this book was essential to its successful completion. I am grateful to those authors who have spent their lives studying Washington and who provided me the books I used as resources. As an amateur military historian I marvel at their expertise and knowledge. That said, the reader should know that while I have done my best to live up to the factual standards demanded by history, if there are any errors of fact or interpretation herein they are my own. Finally, although at the time of this writing I work at a major corporation and teach at a university, the writing and views represented within are also my own and in no way reflect any official position of either organization.

# GEORGE
# WASHINGTON
*and the*
# ART OF
# BUSINESS

# Introduction

*Why George Washington?*

You, the reader, might be excused for asking why someone would choose to write a book titled *George Washington and the Art of Business: Leadership Principles of America's First Commander-in-Chief.* You would note that George Washington was primarily a general and a politician, not a business leader. Besides, we know essentially everything about him: he was the Father of our Country, led our troops during the Revolution, crossed the Delaware, and so on. What principles could we learn that we don't already know?

In truth, many of us know George Washington's achievements but little of how he brought them about. Washington's accomplishments put him in a class that few other leaders in history can match. He created an army essentially from nothing and used it to defeat the leading power of Europe, winning independence for his country. He then went on to become the first president of the United States by unanimous vote of the electoral college. As Thomas Jefferson said of him, "For his was the singular destiny and merit, of leading the armies of his country successfully through an arduous war, for the establishment of its independence; of conducting its councils through the birth of a government, new in its forms and principles, until it had settled down into a quiet and orderly train; and of scrupulously obeying the laws through the whole of his career, civil and military, of which the history of the world furnishes no other example." Obviously, a person who has accomplished those feats is one from whom we can learn a great deal about leadership. To do so requires a better understanding of how George Washington developed the leadership traits and skills that were the source of his success. This book provides that understanding and seeks to go beyond it to show how those same capabilities can be applied in business to achieve success.

In his youth Washington developed a strong sense of self-discipline that would shape his character and allow him in later life to channel his energy into positive results. He developed a passion for knowledge that would serve him well in learning how to be a surveyor of the new land, a businessman who saw the promise of that land, a warrior who would fight to free it, and a president who would lay the foundations of its greatness. Washington's character included great courage, both physical and moral. His physical courage would see him through many battles and inspire his men. His moral courage and integrity would lead others to trust him with great power, knowing he would use it for the common good and not his own.

As he aged and gained wisdom, Washington developed a vision of what America could become. During the trials of war he was chosen by Congress to be the colonies' highest-ranking general. As such Washington had to develop a strategy that would somehow equalize the great imbalance of military power between the colonies and Great Britain and achieve the goal of independence. Beyond creating a strategy, Washington had to execute it, and do so within the limitations of military and political systems that were not just in their infancy but being created on the fly. Those seeking to thwart him included not only Great Britain and its Loyalists in the colonies. There were those in the Rebellion who were jealous of Washington and sought any opportunity to criticize him in order to elevate themselves.

Washington was able to lead the colonies to independence because he had the ability to persuade and inspire others, to include others in the decision-making process, to develop a strong intelligence-gathering system, to seize opportunities wherever they arose, to persevere when setbacks (and there were many) occurred, and to learn from his mistakes.

Although his achievements are the stuff of legend, Washington was far from being a god. He made his share of errors in judgment, resulting in lost battles that would bring his nation's cause to the edge of defeat. He could misjudge people with terrible consequences. Though most of the time very self-disciplined, he could lose his temper and show great anger. We will look at these flaws and mistakes in this book and come to understand how, despite them, he achieved so much.

Each chapter in the book covers a key period in Washington's life, in roughly chronological order. Within each chapter his actions are discussed and the important leadership principles they illustrate are described. These are augmented by examples from modern business to reinforce the points made.

Washington's character and career, though not flawless, stand in stark contrast to the self-promotion, selfishness, and lack of integrity of too many of today's business leaders, sports stars, and celebrities. Fisher Ames, in his eulogy of Washington, said, "His preeminence is not so much to be seen in the display of any one virtue as in the possession of them all, and in the practice of the most difficult. Hereafter, therefore, his character must be studied as a model, a precious one to a free republic." My hope is that by examining how Washington's traits and skills translated into great achievements and seeing how this model can be applied to modern business, the reader will be both instructed by his methods and inspired by his example.

# 1 ▪ Character

## *The Foundation of Washington's Leadership Principles*

We can only imagine the many and various feelings coursing through George Washington as he bade farewell to his dinner guests the evening of March 3, 1797. This was his last day as the first president of the newly formed United States of America. As he raised his glass in a toast saying, "Ladies and gentlemen, this is the last time I shall drink your health as a public man," Washington could look back at a long career that included great victories and devastating defeats. Washington had had to overcome the death of his father at a young age, defeats in his first military ventures, numerous illnesses (including smallpox, malaria, and dysentery) that would nearly kill him, another series of early losses in the Revolutionary War, and various intrigues against him while he served in leadership positions. Through his career he had surmounted these challenges, capping his public service by winning the war for independence and presiding over the birth of a new nation and political system. Marked by momentous highs and deep lows, Washington's career was a long struggle for a great cause in which he had fully invested his heart, mind, and soul. Through his skill, wisdom, and perseverance Washington had laid the groundwork for the fulfillment of his vision for America.

Although on a less epic scale, there is a parallel between Washington and his life and those of us who work in today's business world. The stakes may not be as high, but we too have visions we seek to fulfill as well as our share of victories and defeats. Each of us must lead others or persuade them to our side to achieve our goals. We all need to be organized, make sound decisions, and implement them. Continual learning is an ongoing focus as are situations that challenge our moral courage and integrity. Given these parallels and Washington's skill at achieving his goals, we can learn much from examining his career and his leadership capabilities. In this chapter we will see the difficulties of Washington's early experiences in leadership and how he reacted to and learned from his failures. Then we will look at modern examples of leadership in business that reflect some of the principles he learned.

### Building Self-Discipline, Integrity, and a Desire to Learn

Born in 1732 in a "new world" that brimmed with promise, George Washington joined a family that was part of the upper echelon in Virginia society but not particularly wealthy. George's father, Augustine Washington, did own property, which was the basis for wealth in those times; however, the amount he owned was not sufficient to make him one of the top men in the colonies. George's mother was Mary Ball, Augustine's second wife, the first having died in 1728. George had five brothers and one sister who lived beyond childhood.

While young George's parents provided the basis for his upbringing and character, his older brother Lawrence became Washington's model, especially as their father died when George was only eleven. Lawrence was fourteen years older than George and a product of Augustine's first marriage. He had been educated in England, served as a military officer in the British Army, and was a member of Virginia's legislature, the House of Burgesses. Lawrence had also married into one of Virginia's elite families, the Fairfaxes, who owned millions of acres of land and held high positions in government. Washington would learn much about being a gentleman and leader by spending time at Lawrence's Mount Vernon estate and Belvoir, the Fairfax manor. There he would see what was expected of men of influence and listen to wise conversations on a variety of topics, thus expanding his education. Equally as important, Washington would learn the need for self-discipline, virtue, proper conduct, and accomplishment.

With this example and mentoring George began modeling himself for achievement at a very young age. He developed a strong sense of self-discipline and love of learning, two key traits that foster success. At age sixteen he copied advice from the "Rules of Civility and Decent Behavior in Company and Conversation"—a list of 110 rules, many of which seem quaint today. They included advice such as "Every action done in Company, ought to be with Some Sign of Respect to those that are Present," "Be no Flatterer," and "Shew not yourself glad at the Misfortune of another though he were your enemy." This type of moral education helped instill in Washington the sense of propriety and integrity that would form his character. Combined with his physical stature (he was roughly 6′ 2″ tall, weighed about 200 pounds, had broad shoulders and a narrow waist, and was very strong), Washington's gentlemanly behavior would add to his dominating presence in any situation.

Washington's education was simple and practical, focused on training him in basic skills and manners. He never attended college and would always rue what he called his "defective education." Besides what he learned in the local school or through his mentors, he was largely self-taught. When he was in his teens he copied many types of business letters and legal papers to learn the ways of commerce. His work tended to be neat and orderly. He also schooled himself in land surveying, a skill needed in the colonies where much of the land was unmapped.

Although studious, Washington was no bookworm. At the same time he was nourishing his mind he was strengthening his body. He played the sports of his day and was very physically active. As he grew older Washington became an excellent horseman, something remarked upon by others during his military campaigns. Thomas Jefferson would later call him "the best horseman of his age."

Washington's first job came at age sixteen. Through Lawrence, George had been taken under the wing of Lord Fairfax. Fairfax owned huge tracts of unsettled land beyond the Blue Ridge Mountains in the Shenandoah Valley and needed them surveyed so they could be sold to settlers. Knowing Washington's character and his training as a surveyor, Lord Fairfax hired young George for the position.

To perform this mission Washington had to learn to rough it in the wilderness. At first he was taken aback by the difference between living on an estate and surviving on the frontier, stating about his bed that "to my surprise I found it to be nothing but a Little Straw-Matted together without Sheets or any thing else but only one thread Bare blanket with double its Weight of Vermin such as Lice Fleas etc." But he soon became skilled at critical survival skills such as navigating in the field, hunting for food, and dealing with the local tribes in the area. He became inured to hardship, learned to think quickly, and developed self-sufficiency. These skills would prove critical when he later took the field as a military officer.

### Physical and Moral Courage

Washington acquitted himself well in his first job and was soon made the public surveyor. At this time he also became involved in an enterprise with Lawrence and other leading men in Virginia to settle the Ohio River Valley. This bountiful area was the natural path of expansion for the British colonies, and the desire to settle this land was strong. However, the move of settlers westward created tensions with the French, who also claimed the Ohio River Valley. War with the French became a distinct possibility, and Washington, being a young gentleman from a leading family, was naturally drawn into Virginia's militia system. There, with the help of Lawrence, he was given rank equivalent to major and at the young age of nineteen became responsible for a military district. Lacking formal training, Washington read military manuals and learned the tactics of the day to prepare for this challenge.

The possibility of conflict with the French over the Ohio territories increased, and at age twenty-two Washington was selected by Virginia's lieutenant governor Robert Dinwiddie for a mission requiring diplomatic, military, and scouting skills. Washington was ordered to meet with the local Indian tribes and ask them to escort him to the French commander (during this time the various tribes might be allied with either the French or the British). Once there he was to deliver a letter demanding to know French intentions. His other mission was to learn all he could about the size of French forces, forts, and capabilities. Washington set out in the middle of November to make his way west, accompanied by a local frontiersman, Christopher Gist. Braving winter conditions, the two men traveled to meet with the tribal chiefs and persuaded them to provide assistance in reaching the French headquarters and delivering the letter. With the mission accomplished, Washington and Gist began their return journey; however, deep snow made travel slow and treacherous. With no fodder available their horses were starving and quickly became too weak to ride. Misfortune struck again when their Indian guide turned on them, shooting at Washington and Gist before he could be subdued. Although Gist wanted to kill the man, Washington set him free. Fearing other hostile Indians were tracking them, they pushed on, coming to a halt at their next obstacle, the Allegheny River. A raft had to be built to float across the icy Allegheny, and as they made their way into the current Washington had the bad fortune of falling off the unstable craft. Cold but undaunted, Washington and Gist reached a small island in the middle of the river where they spent the night. Luckily, it was so cold that the next morning they were able to walk across the totally frozen river to the shore. When Washington finally returned to civilization he shared his observations with the lieutenant governor, telling him that it was the French intention to move into the Ohio Valley with troops to secure it for their own. Washington would soon find himself in the middle of skirmishes and battles between these two expanding empires.

Dinwiddie raised troops to meet the threat and protect British interests in the west. Although offered command of the entire expedition, Washington turned it down, knowing himself to be still a neophyte at military affairs. Instead, he was made second in command of these forces and was to lead the advance party of 250 men to prepare the way for the main force. The objective of this small army was to reinforce a British fort under construction on the Ohio River.

As he was moving forward Washington heard that the French had forced the surrender of the fort and were in the area with roughly 1,000 men. In addition, there were rumors of 600 Chippewa and Ottawa warriors coming to reinforce the French. Washington, outnumbered in the extreme, far in advance of supporting troops, and leading untrained militia, knew his situation was dire. His response was to bring together the leaders in his small force in a "council of war."

Calling a council of war would be a tactic Washington would employ throughout his military career—a leadership and decision-making style of inclusion. In these councils Washington would elicit the opinions of the various leaders, allow debate, and then make his decision. This approach is discussed later in more detail, as it was a cornerstone of Washington's leadership. The council determined that the best move would be to advance closer to the fort by marching to an Ohio Company storehouse, which they would fortify while awaiting reinforcements.

As they moved deeper into the wilderness, they realized that they were being shadowed by a small group of French scouts. Seeking to seize an opportunity to attack the enemy, Washington found the enemy encampment, and near a place called Great Meadows he launched a surprise attack. Braving bullets in which one man standing close to him was killed and three were wounded, Washington led his force to kill ten of the enemy and capture twenty-one. Unfortunately, one of the enemy escaped, bringing word of the small force to the French fort.

Washington now faced another dilemma: to advance or retreat. Knowing he would be attacked by the larger French force, he decided to fortify his camp at Great Meadows and await reinforcements. He called his outpost Fort Necessity. More troops did arrive, but their commander was uncooperative and the men were poorly trained. As these men served to reduce further the limited amount of food available at the camp, they were more trouble than help. Bad luck struck again when, hearing of an impending French attack, Washington's Indian allies deserted him. Then, in the first days of July 1754, the French force of about 500 men, augmented by several hundred warriors, reached Fort Necessity.

The French advanced on the fort on the morning of July 3, skirmishing with Washington's troops. As the fighting continued, a heavy rain came, drenching Washington's men and rendering many of their weapons useless. The situation was grim. At roughly eight in the evening the French requested a parley to demand the fort's surrender. Washington, recognizing his position as untenable, accepted the proffered documents and signed them. The paper, written in French, would soon come back to haunt him. The next day Washington led his men out of Fort Necessity, leaving it to the French. His men were discouraged, but sharing their trials and tribulations as well as showing confidence with his own demeanor, their leader brought them to a place named Wills' Creek. There they found food and safety. Washington rode on to make a report to Dinwiddie and the Virginia legislature, which, understanding the situation, voted thanks to Washington and his men for their bravery and sacrifice.

Unfortunately, the document Washington had signed in haste claimed that in his attack at Great Meadows he had "assassinated" a French diplomat. This "admission" would cause great consternation in Europe and sully Washington's name overseas. Fort Necessity proved to be the first of his defeats and it would not be his last. However, after both Fort Necessity and his future lost battles, Washington would always be able to persevere and rebound.

During this time when Washington was learning his military skills, Lawrence died. As a result, Washington became responsible for supervising Mount Vernon, which in the future would become well known as his home. Frustrated with a decision by

Governor Dinwiddie* that denied him his proper rank in the reorganized Virginia militia, Washington left military service and returned to Mount Vernon to restart his civilian career as a businessman. It would be a short retirement, for in 1755 the British government decided to attack the French to secure their claims in the new world.

Although war had not formally been declared between France and Britain the main objective of the British military plan in North America was to drive the French out of disputed British lands, including the Ohio River Valley. The key to the valley was Fort Duquesne. To achieve this objective British major-general Edward Braddock was tasked with leading the effort. Braddock, although not practiced at frontier warfare, was a solid trainer of troops and organizer of campaigns. He was able to orchestrate resources in men and supplies that had not been possible in previous campaigns against the French. These included not just militia but regular British troops, well trained, disciplined, and practiced in the art of formal European warfare. Washington, watching these preparations, could not restrain himself from volunteering for the expedition. Likely seeing the campaign as an opportunity to learn more of the military art and a chance to rectify his loss at Fort Necessity by defeating the French in battle, he became an unpaid aide to Braddock.

As Washington saw the British troops assembling at Fort Cumberland in preparation of moving west, his frontier experience told him there would be problems. Although a young "provincial," Washington had the moral courage to tell Braddock that given his knowledge of the territory they would cross, he knew the British columns would be heavily encumbered and slowed by all their attendant baggage. Braddock, not knowing the country but believing these accoutrements necessary for traditional warfare, chose not to listen to the young man. Only after struggling through the wilderness for days did Braddock realize that he was

---

*Dinwiddie was the lieutenant governor, but as governors were mostly absent at this time, he was de facto governor. In many books he is referred to as "governor."

perhaps right and asked him for advice. Washington, understanding Fort Duquesne to be weakly held but with French reinforcements on the way, wanted to take advantage of the short window of opportunity. Therefore he advised Braddock to split his army into two forces. One group was to continue to push through the woods with the baggage train while the other, carrying only what was necessary for battle, was to move quickly to attack the fort. Braddock agreed and the plan was put in motion.

Unfortunately, the mobile force was not as mobile as hoped. Again, used to European warfare, they moved excruciatingly slowly, progressing only twelve miles in four days. It had taken the army a month to march only 100 miles, but finally, on July 8, 1755, they were in a position to attack the fort the next day.

The plan was to push forward with British troops and two six-pound cannon in advance of the army. Offering an alternative plan, Washington suggested to Braddock that Virginia rangers, colonial light troops used to backwoods fighting, screen the movement toward the fort. He felt these troops, used to bush fighting and scouting, were more capable than the British regulars of protecting the main force from a surprise attack. Braddock, believing in the superiority of his troops, rejected the suggestion. Instead he formed his troops according to his plan and initiated the march on July 9. Washington accompanied the general's party.

Around mid-afternoon heavy gunfire could be heard in the area of the advance guard. As Washington had feared, they had been surprised by a combined French-Indian force attacking from the woods. Unnerved by the unexpected attack, frightened by the fierce war cries of the warriors, and fighting an enemy they could not see, the advance party fell apart. Running back toward the main force they created confusion and consternation in that body as well. Braddock attempted to rally his troops, forming them into line to fire back into the woods. Washington urged him to spread his men out like the Virginia rangers, moving in the woods to fight Indian-style. But Braddock would have none of it, instead forcing his men to do battle in European style. Meanwhile the fighting continued to intensify.

Washington, carrying orders for Braddock, served with conspicuous gallantry. Many bullets went through his coat, and two horses were shot beneath him. At one point, to stop an enemy advance, he dismounted to fire one of the cannon at the enemy. However, neither Braddock's or Washington's efforts nor those of the brave British officers were effective. The British troops were shot down where they stood until the regular troops folded and the battle became a rout. Many were killed and scalped as they tried to flee the battlefield. The scattered remnants of Braddock's army regrouped only after they crossed the Monongahela River, their losses in killed and wounded numbering almost 800 officers and men. Braddock himself was among the casualties, having been mortally wounded in the battle. To assist the army in recovering, Washington was sent to the rear to bring help, returning the next day with supplies. The army finally retreated on July 13 to Great Meadows, ironically the scene of Washington's first defeat. It was there that Braddock succumbed to his wounds and at his funeral Washington led the ceremony.

Washington returned to Mount Vernon somewhat bitter from his military experiences. In a letter to relatives he made clear his frustration with the British regulars, of which so much had been expected. "The dastardly behavior of those they called regulars exposed all others, that were ordered to do their duty, to almost certain death, and at last, in despite of all efforts of the officers to the contrary, they ran as sheep pursued by dogs and it was impossible to rally them." He also looked askance at his earlier military experiences on the frontier, saying in a letter to his brother, "I was then appointed, with trifling pay, to conduct a handful of men to the Ohio. What did I get by that? Why, after putting myself to a considerable expense in equipping and providing necessaries for the campaign, I went out, was soundly beaten and lost all. . . . I then went out a volunteer with General Braddock and lost all my horses and many other things. But this being a voluntary act I ought not to have mentioned it, nor should I have done it, were it not to show that I have been on the losing order ever since I entered the service."

Although downcast with his string of defeats and losses, Washington persevered in the service of his country despite entreaties from his mother not to persist in military service. Washington's sense of honor required him to serve if asked. Indeed he was asked, being offered command of all the Virginia forces to defend the colony. His ability to carry on after losing would mark his later career and be one of his principles of success.

Washington's first act was to improve the discipline and training of the militia, which he knew was one of the major reasons for prior defeats. One specific area of focus was Indian-style bush fighting, an essential skill for the type of frontier fighting that took place in the colonies. Washington also changed the uniforms of his men from European style to a lighter frontier style modeled after Indian warrior dress. He ordered forts constructed at strategic places and roads built to improve the army's ability to defend them. He had learned from prior campaigns and understood that the organization of the armed forces was crucial to success.

However, despite his best efforts, Washington's improvements were blocked by Governor Dinwiddie. The governor was likely jealous of Washington's reputation and had preferred another political favorite to command Virginia's troops. This jealousy, combined with Dinwiddie's opinion that his own military skills were the equal of Washington's, led the governor to countermand many of Washington's orders and in general treat him very poorly. Washington eventually became so frustrated it made him physically ill, and for a short time he had to return to Mount Vernon to recover. It may surprise us today to learn that Washington, who now has such a large place in American history, had to suffer the same "bad boss" problems many of us have experienced. However, at this early stage of his career, young Washington was still at a point that he had to put up with Dinwiddie's machinations and interference with no recourse.

War between France and Britain was formally declared in 1756, and the conflict would be known in North America as the French-Indian War. In 1758 the British remounted their efforts to drive the French from the Ohio River Valley, and Virginia's forces were going to be part of that effort. Washington desperately wanted to be involved, so he hastened to return to service. The goal again was Fort Duquesne, and for a third time Washington rode forth to attempt its capture. The British forces moved glacially but eventually came to within fifty miles of the fort. Brigadier General John Forbes, the army's commander, sent ahead a detachment of 800 men. Washington advised against this, believing it would give up the advantage of surprise. As he had predicted, the advance guard did indeed give the fort warning. In addition, the French launched an attack on them, driving them back to the main force with huge losses.

Forbes, recognizing he needed another approach, gave Washington command of the advance guard, and the army proceeded forward. Amazingly, arriving at Fort Duquesne they found it abandoned and in ruins. Its commander, knowing the British were nearby and that he would not receive reinforcements, had blown up his arsenal and torched the fort. General Forbes rebuilt the stronghold and named it Fort Pitt in honor of the prime minister of England, William Pitt (as you may have guessed the town that grew around the fort eventually became the major metropolis of Pittsburgh). Washington had finally achieved success in his military career. More important, with this and other British victories, by 1763 peace was declared and the French threat was eliminated from the colonies.

### Innovation and Attention to Detail

Now in his late twenties, Washington retired to civilian life for a second time. He married the young widow Martha Custis in 1759. Martha brought with her two children and a sizable fortune to add to his already considerable holdings (ironically, the Father of our Country would never have biological children of his own but he was very fond of and provided well for Martha's). Washington also took a seat in Virginia's House of Burgesses that had been awaiting the closure of his military activities.

He now turned his talents to running the business of his estate and Virginia politics. In the former he brought an exactness and skill for organization he had begun in his youth and developed in his military years. He would start his day early, having a frugal meal while reading over accounts and correspondence. He would then inspect various parts of his estate, often giving direction on projects and not being afraid to get his own hands dirty in the process. This was followed by a mid-afternoon lunch, again very Spartan. Then in the afternoons Washington would do paperwork or see visitors until dark. This was a routine he would follow both before and after the Revolutionary War.

As a surveyor and farmer, Washington saw the potential value of land. He bought additional parcels of property near Mount Vernon, eventually expanding the estate's acreage from 2,300 to almost 8,000 acres. Mount Vernon's facilities would eventually include a grist mill, a blacksmith shop, a small clothing factory, fisheries, and even a distillery.

Although he was extremely pragmatic and not generally thought of today as an innovator, Washington introduced several ideas to improve his operations. These included moving away from tobacco to wheat as a cash crop before others saw the wisdom of doing so, practicing crop rotation to improve soil fertility, limiting soil erosion by cross plowing, using planned breeding to improve his herds, setting time standards to complete tasks, and modifying implements to increase productivity. After the Revolutionary War, upon receiving the gift of a donkey from the king of Spain and one from Lafayette, Washington embarked on a program to breed donkeys with horses that resulted in the American mule. His purpose was to create a stronger animal for farm work. Success in this arena led to Washington being an early promoter of the mule over the horse for farm work and to his becoming known not only as the "Father of Our Country" but also the "Father of the American Mule." Although not all these expansions and innovations came before the Revolutionary War, they are all excellent examples of Washington as a businessman.

The result of his innovation and attention to detail was increased output (wheat output at Mount Vernon grew from 257 bushels to 6,241 between 1765 and 1770), well-known quality (it was said that any barrel of flour with the Washington brand was exempted from inspection in West Indian ports), and increasing revenues.

## Integrity and Leadership in Business

The idea of a young Washington copying down maxims from the "Rules of Civility and Decent Behavior" might make us smile today, but the self-discipline and self-improvement he demonstrated are still essential for business success. We know that to win customers and lead others ethically, business leaders need to be trustworthy, organized, and confident; project the right image; and constantly work to improve themselves. This desire for self-improvement has created a multibillion-dollar industry that provides advice on a myriad of ways to succeed. While some of that advice is faddish—or worse, unethical—much (such as *The 7 Habits of Highly Effective People*) can offer great insight into how to be better leaders and professionals. Like *The 7 Habits,* the best of these guides focus their advice on the need for strong character and integrity.

One of the most amazing modern-day cases of a lack of moral courage and integrity occurred not in business (which has had its share of moral shortcomings) but in a psychological experiment performed in 1973 on seminary students. One half of the aspiring pastors were told to prepare a sermon on the Good Samaritan, the story in which a traveler stops to help someone in need. The other half were given a different topic unrelated to helping others in need. Then each student was told one of three things: (1) the student was late and needed to rush to another building to deliver the sermon (high-hurry situation), (2) he was on time and should go now to present the sermon (intermediate-hurry), or (3) he had a few minutes to spare but might as well go over now. On the way to the other building the student had to go through an alley in which a homeless man was sitting. As the student passed, the man would cough and groan. If the student stopped to provide assistance the homeless man would allow him to do so; otherwise, the man was not to ask for any help. As part of the experiment each student was rated on the level of help he provided. The findings were shocking, as many of the students did not stop to help the man in need. The seminary students in a hurry were much less likely to help than were the others. Also, those students giving the sermon on the need to help others were no more likely to provide assistance to the homeless man than those who were giving a sermon on another topic. These two findings make the point that not only can our behavior differ greatly from what we profess, but that outside pressure (in this case, being a little late) reduces the probability that we will stick to our principles, even if we have the best of intentions. Obviously, it is not enough for leaders to talk about doing the right thing; they must strive every day to live up to the standards they espouse.

We have seen that Washington learned his new jobs at a young age, and in business there are many stories of successful executives and managers who started their careers learning the business from the bottom up. Dan Cathy, president of the Chick-fil-A Company, began his training at age nine when he sang in his father's restaurants to entertain customers. After college he was hired by his father, S. Truett (founder of Chick-fil-A), to be the director of operations for the company. In that job he was responsible for opening fifty restaurants around the country. This enabled him to be very focused on the details as well as strategy. He can still go in the kitchen of any restaurant to make any of the recipes and will ensure all the restaurants are clean, even to the point of busing tables. Chick-fil-A has grown to be a $1.5 billion business, was ranked number 17 on the list of Top 50 restaurant chains in 2003, and has received *Restaurants & Institutions* magazine's Customer Satisfaction Award. Cathy believes the key to customer satisfaction is treating employees right, saying, "The way you treat people internally is what drives the customers' emotional response back to the business." Continual learning is also a major factor in Dan's and Chick-fil-A's success. One restaurant operator said of him, "Dan operates on a different level than most of us. He's a big-picture thinker. He's definitely very well-read and has a great feel for our industry and where it's headed, and how we can enhance our position in the marketplace."

Often in his early career Washington showed his impulse to gain as much learning as possible, and in today's competitive world it's imperative to have a thirst for learning and to nourish it. As Washington proved, this can be done through determining the skills to acquire and achieving mastery through self-education. Daily learning can be accomplished through reading, on topics specific to your industry or skill as well as on others that seem unrelated. It is often from non-business areas that you can gain valuable insights. Some people find useful analogies from sports, the military, theater, philosophy, biology—the possibilities are endless. Actually, this book is an example of this approach, as it provides business insights from Washington's life and career.

Throughout his early military career Washington had behaved with integrity and courage, both physical and moral. It's the rare business leadership position today that requires physical courage; however, moral courage is essential. Norm Brodsky, who owns a storage company in New York City and sidelines as a writer for *Inc.* magazine, provides a good example of moral courage and how it can pay off from both a business and personal standpoint. Brodsky was contemplating instituting drug testing at his company but was hesitant. Personally he'd used marijuana in his youth and therefore felt somewhat hypocritical in testing others for drug use. From a business perspective he knew he'd lose some employees and was concerned he'd have trouble replacing them in an increasingly tight labor market. In addition, there would be the emotional strain of releasing long-term employees as well as the cost to implement the testing itself. Yet fear of work accidents eventually drove Brodsky to enact the testing.

In addition to testing new hires and 130 current employees, Brodsky himself as well as his family members who worked at the business all submitted to the testing. This showed that Brodsky was not only serious about the new policy but that he was willing to subject himself to the testing's invasive nature, just as he required his lowest-ranked employee to do.

The first days of testing the current workforce confirmed Brodsky's worst fears; about half of his employees were failing the test. The first round served to put employees on notice that they needed to become drug free; they were not dismissed immediately. Everyone that Brodsky talked to promised that he or she would pass the next test, but only one employee did so: Bruce Howard. In the end Brodsky lost a quarter of his current employees for drug usage.

Although replacing his losses took time, the payoff was worth it. Accident rates and petty theft declined significantly, and insurance rates and worker compensation costs soon followed. More important, the workers who remained were thankful for a better and safer work environment, which helped Brodsky retain these more valuable employees. Finally, on a personal level, Bruce Howard used the wake-up call of the drug test to turn his life around, not only passing the drug test but going on to become one of Brodsky's top supervisors. He said, "I came to a crossroads. . . . I changed my whole life. I became a more focused and serious person because, you know, you get rid of the distortion that comes from smoking weed. And I've never regretted making that choice. My life is better now in every way."

In both his early experiences with military command and in developing his farm at Mount Vernon, Washington proved himself an innovator. All businesspeople know that innovation is crucial to success. Many people today rightly point to Southwest Airlines as a company whose innovative business model enables them to price tickets below their competitors and increase market share. However, pricing innovation in the airline industry can be traced back even earlier to the 1940s. Back then, Juan Trippe, founder of Pan American Airlines, introduced the two-tier pricing strategy of expensive first-class travel and cheaper "tourist" travel in the same plane, fueling Pan Am's rapid growth.

Another example of innovation is from the area of professional sports. Much of today's professional sports approach of having every second of a game filled with nonstop entertainment originated with promotional wizard Bill Veeck. Veeck, whose father was president of the Chicago Cubs, began working in baseball in 1925 at the age of eleven, selling tickets and popcorn as well as performing grounds-keeping chores. At age nineteen he left college to become treasurer for the Cubs, and at age twenty-seven he bought his first baseball franchise, the American Association Milwaukee team. There he began his career-long list of stunts by giving away pets, allowing couples to wed in the ballpark, and having morning games for people who worked nights. Veeck also applied his talents to running the club, which won three pennants. After selling his team for a tidy profit, Veeck went on to own the Cleveland Indians, St. Louis Browns, and Chicago White Sox. His other innovations included allowing fans to vote on when to bunt, steal, or change pitchers, bringing the first African American player to the American League, putting in the first scoreboard with fireworks, having ballplayers tip their hats after home runs, and having "Take Me Out to the Ball Game" sung during the seventh-inning stretch. Veeck's showmanship resulted in outstanding attendance records and great ticket sales, and his reputation for groundbreaking innovations won Veeck membership in baseball's Hall of Fame in 1991.

Another innovator who focuses on details is thoroughbred trainer D. Wayne Lukas. As of 2004 Lukas was tied for the most wins in Triple Crown races, had the most wins (seventeen) for the prestigious Breeders' Cup series, and earned the most money of any trainer in fourteen different years (his lifetime earnings are double that of any other trainer). Lukas's most important innovation was to change the industry rules by taking his horses anyplace in the United States where they could win. Previously the tradition-bound horse racing trainers would only race locally, thinking their horses were too fragile to travel far from home to win. In an interview with *Harvard Business Review* Lukas explained his philosophy: his horses' owners were expecting to win, and to enable them to do so Lukas would fly his thoroughbreds to lesser tracks around the country if they stood a good chance of winning there. The results were higher earnings, satisfied owners, and a burgeoning reputation.

The other key to Lukas's success is attention to detail. It starts with a strenuous schedule that includes eighteen-hour days every day of the year. Lukas focuses on everything from horse selection, which is the foundation of winning, to seemingly small things such as the color of his bridles (he introduced unique white bridles to draw attention to his horses), how his assistants answer the phone, and the cleanliness of his stables. Lukas provides this viewpoint to employees: "I think the discipline you develop outside the barn and the discipline you develop in your life will carry over into the discipline I need from you in handling the horses and in the stalls. We keep our barns spotless not because a horse will run any faster if the barn is absolutely spotless but because that discipline will carry over to what does make a difference." Although Lukas is rightly proud of his winning record he believes his real legacy will be the assistant trainers to whom he has taught the intricacies of the industry, eleven of whom have gone on to achieve their own success.

## Summary

In the short space of less than thirty years Washington now had the foundation for his leadership style and his future career. He had developed an inner core of *self-discipline*, had shown *courage* on the battlefield, and had developed a strong reputation for *integrity*. Washington's *desire to always keep learning* allowed him to master specific skills such as backwoods survival, business acumen, military proficiency, and political wisdom that proved he was not only honest but capable. At his Mount Vernon estate his *innovation and attention to detail* made him a successful and wealthy businessman. Together, these character traits and skills were the essential elements that would create a level of trust and confidence that would make Washington's fellow countrymen willing to follow him in the trials to come.

Washington had also learned one other important thing—the profound fact that the British Army could be beaten. As Benjamin Franklin said about the Braddock debacle, "This whole transaction gave us the first suspicion that our exalted ideas of the prowess of British regular troops had not been well-founded."

Last, this time in Washington's life not only molded his leadership style but also showed him the great promise and potential of the vast new land. The latter sparked in Washington's imagination the beginning vision of what the small colonies could someday become. It would be this vision that would inspire him to persevere during the coming Revolutionary War and his presidency.

# 2 ▪ A Rough Beginning
## Organizing a Revolution

As a wealthy businessman and respected legislator, Washington watched with keen interest the British efforts to control the trade of the colonies and raise revenues by taxing them. Although a loyal subject of the crown, Washington, like many of his peers, looked askance at new British laws such as the Stamp Act. Not only were these taxes unpopular but the idea that the British government could tax the colonists without their consent was alarming in the extreme. So, despite his prior loyalties, Washington strongly supported the 1765 Virginia House of Burgesses' resolutions to the home country denouncing the taxes and the infringement on the colonists' rights. As a result of protestations such as these the British government repealed the Stamp Act, and thus some goodwill with the colonies was reestablished. However, full reconciliation was incomplete as the British government still reserved the right to tax the colonies, and it put new taxes in place. One major center of discontent was Boston, where leaders continued to petition for the rights of the colonists. As tensions increased, two regiments of British troops were sent to silence the dissent, but these strong-arm tactics only added fuel to the fire. On March 5, 1770, violence erupted between the populace and the British regulars when the troops were threatened by a mob and responded by firing into the crowd. The "Boston Massacre" left four dead and others wounded, but more important, further increased the rift between the colonies and the mother country.

George Washington and others had hoped that a military conflict could be avoided by an economic boycott of British goods, and indeed this strategy met with some success. All taxes were lifted except the tax for tea, that one being kept to maintain the British right of taxation. So the taxation issue still remained a source of dispute between the Mother Country and the colonies. To challenge this policy, all colonial harbors refused to unload the tea ships of England's premier firm, the East India Company. Boston, of course, went one step further. A small party of citizens dressed as Indians boarded the ships and threw the tea overboard. This act of defiance enraged the British government and elicited a sharp and prompt response. Parliament decreed that the port of Boston was to be closed to all trade on June 1, 1774. The other colonies, seeing the harsh treatment of Massachusetts, were now thoroughly aroused. Military preparations commenced, and in an act of solidarity each colony's legislature made plans to convene in a General Congress, the first of its kind in the colonies.

Washington had by now given up hope of persuading Britain by economic means. In response to a letter from a friend who spoke of advising one more petition to Parliament, Washington wrote back, "But have we not tried this already? Have we not addressed the lords and remonstrated to the commons? And to what end? Does it not appear as clear as the sun in its meridian brightness that there is a regular, systematic plan to fix the right and practice of taxation upon us? . . . Is not the attack upon the liberty and property of the people of Boston . . . a plain and self-evident proof of what they are aiming at? . . . Ought we not, then, to put our virtue and fortitude to the severest tests?"

With such views, Washington was selected as one of Virginia's representatives to the General Congress that was to meet in Philadelphia. At this congress Washington impressed his fellow delegates not with a quick wit or his speaking skills but with the strength of his wisdom. The congress met for fifty-one days and affirmed its dismay over the treatment of Boston. Furthermore, the congress restated the expected rights of the colonies and resolved their wish for a fair resolution of the issues and reconciliation with Britain. Left unspoken was the next step if the reconciliation failed, and that was war.

The war was soon in coming as events in Boston quickly spiraled out of control. British general Thomas Gage, commander of the Boston garrison, was ordered to stamp out the rebellion in Massachusetts before it could spread to other colonies. To do so he decided to launch a quick expedition into the countryside to round up rebel politicians such as Sam Adams and John Hancock as well as destroy arms depots the local militias were building. The force was to be led by Lieutenant Colonel Francis Smith, and second in command was Major Thomas Pitcairn of the Royal Marines. It was Pitcairn who had written to Lord Sandwich, British secretary of state, that "I am satisfied that one active campaign, a smart action, and burning two or three of their towns, will set everything to rights." The letter was forwarded to King George, who agreed heartily with his opinion. Pitcairn was now to have the opportunity to test his theory.

Late in the evening of April 18, 1775, roughly 700 British regulars left Boston to execute this mission. Dawn found Pitcairn and the advance guard of the detachment in the small town of Lexington, facing seventy Massachusetts militiamen. Pitcairn yelled, "Disperse, ye Rebels! Lay down your arms and disperse." Shots rang out, followed by a British volley, and the militia were scattered. Eight Americans were dead and ten wounded; they would not be the last casualties that day.

The British moved on to Concord where they destroyed rebel supplies, then proceeded to execute a triumphal return to Boston. It was not to be. American militiamen, fighting Indian-style, shot at the retreating British troops as they marched back along the road. The British regiments would try to drive off the Americans but would disperse them only to find them reforming once the British returned to the highway. The retreat soon turned into a rout. Reinforced by a relief force sent from Boston the bloodied detachment was finally able to reach the city, but not until it had taken over 270 casualties.

News of Lexington and Concord soon spread throughout the colonies, further fanning the flames of rebellion. In Massachusetts itself the militia was called out and thousands of men were sent to perform a siege of Boston. Fortifications were built on Breed's Hill across the river from Boston to hem the British in.

Seeing the newly built American lines, on June 17 the new British commander, General William Howe, decided to launch an assault on the Americans and drive them away from the city. He rejected a plan by General Henry Clinton to land in the Americans' rear and cut them off while Howe attacked them from the front. Instead, Howe, wanting to move quickly, chose just to launch the frontal assault on the American redoubt. At 2:00 P.M. British troops began landing around Charlestown, and soon they were moving up the hill. Weighed down by their heavy packs and sweating in the ninety degree heat, the British troops moved slowly toward the American position. The Americans held their fire until the Redcoats were very close, then unleashed three volleys in rapid succession. The British troops, stunned, beat a hasty retreat down the hill, leaving many dead and wounded on the slope. After reassembling his men, Howe launched another attack, only to have it beaten back as well. Finally, only after bringing in reinforcements were Howe's men able to capture the American position. The Battle of Bunker Hill (curiously named as the battle was indeed fought on Breed's Hill) resulted in a British victory but one that was extremely expensive. Howe's army suffered over 1,000 casualties. One of the British dead was Major Pitcairn himself. The Americans, fighting from within the fortifications, suffered less than half that number. Furthermore, the American militia had stood up well against the British regulars, and that served to further the rebellion's cause. Clearly, Pitcairn's theory that forceful action would crush the rebellion was false.

## Organizing the Army

After the action at Lexington and Concord a second congress was convened in May. One of its first acts was to form a union of the states to present a united front on what was quickly becoming a full-fledged war with Britain. This included raising troops, building forts, and coining money. Washington was again a delegate from Virginia and in recognition of his military background was put in charge of all the committees dealing with military matters. As the siege of Boston continued and the possibility of wider conflict grew, it became clear that a commander-in-chief of all American forces would need to be named. There was disagreement between the Southerners and the New Englanders over who should be in command, with the former supporting Washington while the latter preferred Artemas Ward from New England. There was great desire that all in congress should be in unanimous agreement on this important issue, especially as there was fear that the military commander might someday choose to become a military tyrant. In the end the desire for unanimity and Washington's reputation for integrity led him to be chosen by ballot with no dissenting votes. Washington told the congress he was honored and humbly said that he did not feel his abilities sufficient to the task: "Mr. President, though I am truly sensible of the high Honour done me, in this Appointment, yet I feel great distress, from a consciousness that my abilities and military experience may not be equal to the extensive and important Trust: However, as the Congress desire it, I will enter upon the momentous duty, and exert every power I possess in their service, and for support of the glorious cause. I beg they will accept my most cordial thanks for this distinguished testimony of their approbation." However, he said he would serve without pay, only turning in a list of his expenses. In today's day and age of self-promotion it may be hard to understand Washington's actions.

Yet those actions were not only a testament to his character. They also went far in convincing others they could trust him with military power and gave him the credibility to take the actions necessary to win what would be a long war.

Looking back from today's vantage point we tend to think of Washington as being quite old when he was leading the revolution, perhaps in his sixties. This is reinforced by our paintings and images of Washington as an older man. Yet when he took command of the American Army, Washington was only forty-three years old. He was in the prime of his life, a strong and vigorous man. He would need that strength for the coming struggle.

Washington now hurried north to take command of the colonial army surrounding Boston, doing so on July 3, 1775. His first act was to visit the units and positions of his new army as well as scout out those of the enemy. Numbering roughly 17,000 men, the American (also known as the Continental) Army was composed of a hodgepodge of militia units from the various colonies. In contrast to the British regulars, the Continental Army was (to put it kindly) of very mixed quality—mostly undisciplined, poorly supplied, with no standards of military drill, no uniform dress, and lacking in basic sanitation. There was no regular supply system. Troops foraged for their own food as there was no ordered manner of collecting and distributing rations. If they were lucky, a militia unit might have their own uniforms, the look determined by their own preferences and sense of military fashion; but many soldiers merely wore the clothes they left home with. Ammunition was limited and artillery was scarce. Washington soon found that he had taken command of something more like an armed mob than an army.

In contrast, the British Army was professional. Officered by Britain's aristocracy, the army was organized into regiments, each with a proud history in battle and rich military traditions. The British Army had an impressive record of victories in European warfare, most recently winning several triumphs in the Seven Years' War on the Continent. Its officers were known for their bravery and its troops for their steadfastness in battle. In addition, to make up a shortage of manpower, Britain would augment its own forces with Hessian mercenaries, so called because many of the troops came from the German state of Hesse-Cassel. As mercenaries, these units were extremely professional and would prove their mettle on the battlefield.

Supporting Britain's land forces was another major military asset, the Royal Navy. The most powerful navy of its day, the Royal Navy could destroy American shipping, blockade or raid colonial ports, and most important, quickly move the Crown's troops to any position along the American coast. The latter advantage would prove to be a great asset in the war.

Even so, the British military machine had its shortcomings. The army's pool of officer candidates was limited to Anglican families with the right political connections; young Catholic men need not apply. Merit did not determine advancement among the officer corps. Instead, an officer's rank was purchased through buying a commission in the regiment, with higher ranks costing more than lower ones and positions in elite regiments costing more than those in regular units. Formal military education was limited, and although the British Army had its share of military geniuses who studied the art, the majority of young officers spent much of their time gambling or drinking.

Enlisted men came from the lower orders of society, and brutal punishments for both minor and major infractions were used to ensure that the men followed orders and maintained their place in formation. Although his lot was a hard one and his pay was minimal, the British soldier's life was balanced somewhat as his basic needs for food, clothing, and shelter were met and he served in a regiment in which he could take pride.

The British Army's strength in discipline, order, and logistics could sometimes translate into the weaknesses of inflexible battle tactics, unoriginal strategic thinking, and large, cumbersome supply trains. Combined with an arrogance bred from the social status of its officer corps, victories in European warfare, and condescension for the colonial forces, these shortcomings formed a mixture Washington could potentially exploit. First he would need to build an army that could withstand the initial blows and win enough victories to hold the American population's support.

Organizing, training, and supplying the Continental Army and maintaining its strength would prove to be among Washington's greatest tasks in the war. The issues he would face were not unlike those of starting a company from the ground up: bringing together people of different backgrounds, setting standards, organizing functions, and forming individuals into a cohesive team so they can take on better-organized and more established competitors. The task would be very difficult, and at times when the army was on the brink of disintegration, would appear impossible. A recurring issue was the expiration of enlistments. As the soldiers tended to enlist in units, entire regiments could disappear overnight if all the men decided not to reenlist. In modern business it would be like having large portions of your sales force or factory workers leave the firm all at once, with no replacements in sight. Often Washington would have only a small fraction of the men the British had. In a letter to a close friend he wrote, "Could I have foreseen what I have experienced and am likely to experience, no consideration upon earth should have induced me to accept this command."

Yet Washington did not quit. Instead, he pushed forward by convincing troops to reenlist and asking for more troops from the New England colonies. To improve the logistical situation, Washington wrote to the congress to recommend the creation of different supply and combat departments within the army and to request funds to buy more supplies. Congress complied by approving the departments and providing $2 million of credit. Washington instituted a standard drill manual, created by a Massachusetts officer, for all infantry training. He also issued a number of "General Orders" to cover discipline, supply, sanitation, and camp rules, and he implemented a reporting system to know the strength and supply status of every unit under his command. To inspire his men, Washington instituted regular church services and used the clergy to link the cause of the rebellion with that of the higher being Washington referred to as "Providence." Last, to create a clearer chain of command, Washington organized the army into three "Grand Divisions," putting each under a major general reporting to him.

These changes began to allow the Continental Army to fight the British on something approaching equal footing. However, although Washington sought to impose order on this fledgling force and would not shy away from some fairly harsh methods of discipline to do so, he was building a very different army from that of his opponent. This would be an army not led by an aristocracy, manned by the dregs of society, and motivated by martial pride. Instead it would be an army of citizens, led by men of standing in the community, and driven to win by the promise of independence and the right of self-government. In many ways it would be unlike any army the world had ever seen. To create this force would be a long and arduous task for Washington, with many setbacks before final victory was achieved.

In the short term, to protect his lines and potentially force the British out of Boston, Washington still lacked one essential item: artillery. Without it he was at a distinct disadvantage defensively should the British attack. Offensively, Washington had no hope of pounding the British lines to force them to withdraw and end their occupation of Boston. At this point, a man named Henry Knox stepped forward to help end Washington's predicament. Knox would prove to be one of Washington's most trusted subordinates and best friends.

Before the war Knox was a bookseller, and books on military history were his passion. An ardent patriot from the beginning (he had witnessed the Boston Massacre and was a volunteer at Bunker Hill), Knox's self-taught military knowledge would be providential for the American cause. Washington first noticed Knox in an inspection of the lines. Impressed with his knowledge of military tactics, Washington soon came to rely on his advice. Knowing the army's lack of artillery was a crucial weakness, Knox suggested bringing the artillery from the recently captured Fort Ticonderoga to Boston. The idea of moving heavy cannon and its attendant ammunition through 300 miles of wilderness in the dead of winter seemed preposterous. Yet having no other options, Washington commissioned Knox as colonel of the artillery and sent him on the mission.

Knox reached Fort Ticonderoga on December 5. There he gathered roughly sixty pieces of artillery and began the long journey back to Boston. Using boats to move the cannon down Lake Champlain, Knox then turned to a heavy sleds pulled by oxen and horses for the rest of the journey. It was a difficult and arduous task and took over fifty days, but in early March Washington had the heavy cannon he needed to take on the British.

Another critical figure to enter Washington's circle at this time was General Nathanael Greene. Greene was born a Quaker and was expected to maintain that sect's tradition of nonviolence and peace. However, he joined the militia in his early thirties and was consequently expelled from his religion. It was as a Rhode Island militia commander that he arrived in Boston to fight the British. On orders from the congress he was named one of eight brigadier generals of the Continental Army. From his first meeting with Washington he captured the commander's confidence, and the bond would be strengthened over time. Washington grew to lean on Greene's advice, support, and optimism throughout the war and ultimately gave him a major command. It was Greene who earlier had developed innovative plans to attack the British in Boston. Washington had wanted to implement them to strike hard at the enemy and rally the populace, but his other generals stood against it in the American councils of war. Directed by the congress to heed the advice of his generals, Washington had no choice but to delay an assault.

Now, however, thanks to Colonel Knox, Washington had the artillery power he needed to drive the British from Boston. And it was important that he do so. An American expedition to take Canada had failed miserably, loyalist Tories were stirring up trouble, and the congress as well as the people were looking for a victory.

Washington's plan was to occupy Dorchester Heights above the city. From this position his artillery could bombard Boston and support an American attack on the city. However, he needed to act quickly and secretly for if the British knew his plans, they could send troops to seize the Heights first. Intricate preparations were made to ensure that once the American troops took the hill they could fortify their position speedily. Since the ground was still frozen, barrels of soil and wooden obstacles were put in carts so these could be quickly moved into place to create fortifications before the British could react. To cover the sound of these preparations and distract the enemy, Washington had Knox engage the British in artillery duels.

The light of a full moon on the evening of March 4, 1776, helped show the way to the 2,000 men sent to erect a small fort and redoubts on the Heights. Eight hundred men provided security while the remainder raised the fortifications. By morning all was in place. General Howe had gone to bed on March 4 seeing nothing on Dorchester Heights. However, upon waking to see it heavily fortified, Howe was amazed, stating, "The rebels have done more work in one night than my whole army would have done in one month."

Howe now faced a dilemma. He could either assault the American position on the Heights and risk another Bunker Hill fiasco or he could evacuate the city. British honor demanded an assault attempt be made, so plans were developed and troops were mustered. However, a terrible storm rolled in on the night of the planned attack, and it had to be abandoned. After suffering a few days of bombardment Howe was forced to evacuate by sea, loading not only his troops but also over 1,000 Tory loyalists. Heavy cannon and other supplies that could not be taken were destroyed; however, many supplies survived and would ultimately be used by the American troops. In late March the first Continental Army units entered Boston, met by a small but very enthusiastic populace. For Washington and the Revolutionary cause, it was a major victory.

### Making Mistakes—and Learning from Them

Washington had achieved a great success, but there was little time for self-congratulation. The British had boarded their ships not to return to England but to regroup for the next attack. Howe could use the Royal Navy to land his men at whatever location would provide the best strategic advantage. The question for Washington was to second-guess the place Howe would choose to do battle and decide how to stop him. His first instincts and strategic analysis told him New York would be Howe's logical target: "Long Island or New York is, in my Opinion, the Place of their Destination." Control of New York would not only give the British control of a major colonial port but also access to the Hudson River, potentially allowing them to separate New York and the upper states from the rest of the colonies. They could also stir up Loyalist support as New York and the surrounding states of New Jersey and Connecticut had sizable Tory contingents. Although the governors of Rhode Island and Connecticut prodded him for troops to protect their states, Washington was determined to keep his army intact. To be in a position to preempt the British, Washington moved the army to New York, personally arriving in the city on April 13, 1776. He worked feverishly with the local commanders to strengthen the city's defenses before the impending invasion.

The British did not keep Washington waiting long. Led again by General Howe and reinforced by additional British and Hessian troops, 30,000 men were landed on Staten Island in July. This was to become their base of operations for their assault on New York City, which at the time was limited to Manhattan. With General Howe was his brother, Admiral Richard "Black Dick" Howe, commander of the powerful British fleet. Not only would the Royal Navy provide the British Army with greater mobility around New York (much of the area was accessible by water) but the ships' guns would also provide cover for any amphibious landings. Just as important, the British ships would be able to cut off the retreat of any American troops that had to cross water to get back to the mainland. As events would prove, Washington's first mistake of this campaign and of the war overall was his decision to defend New York City proper. General Charles Lee, second in rank only to Washington in the Continental Army and previous commander of the forces around New York, had questioned Washington's ability to hold the town itself, saying, "What to do with the city, I own puzzles me, it is so encircl'd with deep navigable water, that whoever commands the sea must command the town." Strategically, it might have been wiser to concede the defense of the city, destroy any facilities that were of military use, and retreat farther north to protect New England. While the initial moves in the battle for New York were playing out, a momentous change had occurred in the political situation. The congress had been meeting in Philadelphia to consider the next steps in the war, and Washington had been invited in May to come for conferences. In support of Washington and the army, Congress had passed laws that stipulated soldiers' terms of enlistment at three years and established a war office. More important, they had considered whether to seek reconciliation with Great Britain or complete independence. As the military commander-in-chief, Washington refrained from making public statements; however, he privately made clear his view that the time to reconcile had passed, given the views of the British Crown and government. Enough members of Congress agreed with Washington to formally adopt a resolution on July 4, 1776, declaring independence from Britain. The news reached Washington and the army on July 6, and he called out the troops to hear it. The declaration was greeted with cheers by the soldiers. Now the ultimate goal they were fighting for was clear: complete independence from Britain.

It was not to be had without a fight, however. With their command of the sea, the British seized the initiative, conducting raids on American outposts and sending frigates up the Hudson River to harass shipping. Washington's army was outnumbered (he had roughly 20,000 men), outgunned (two out of every ten men did not even have muskets), and essentially immobile (not only did he lack ships to move his men but he had no cavalry to scout or reinforce endangered positions). Just as critically, Washington lacked solid military intelligence about the enemy's intentions. In the previous Boston campaign he had had a steady stream of intelligence from informers and cavalry scouting reports to help him discern his opponent's plans. In New York, there was no such system.

Washington himself was in a difficult position. His generals were of the opinion that evacuating the city was the best course of action. However, Washington had been ordered to defend New York by the congress. He also knew the psychological implications for the army and the people of giving up the city without a defense. Last, Washington understood that doing so would provide the British government more popular support in Britain for the war. As a result the commander felt he had no choice but to make the best of the situation. His strategy was based on a mixture of leveraging his army's strengths and his estimation of his opponent's weaknesses. Americans were good at digging trenches and building defensive works. Thus Washington would strengthen his fortifications and hope that Howe would launch head-on assaults against them. Given Howe's prior lack of creative tactics at Bunker Hill in Boston, Washington felt that he could at a minimum impose huge casualties on the British Army, thereby reducing Britain's willingness to carry on the war.

Washington's strategic plan was soon put to the test. On August 22, British troops, supported by the Royal Navy, landed on Long Island. Lacking good intelligence and believing this to be a feint, Washington sent only a few thousand troops to reinforce his units already on Long Island. In reality, this was General Howe's main thrust, and he had a force of about 22,000 men with which to attack the roughly 10,000 Americans.

This was not the only disadvantage of the Continental Army on Long Island. The current commander, Nathanael Greene, had become ill. His replacement, John Sullivan, agreed with Washington to move 3,000 of Greene's troops farther south to make a stand on Long Island Heights. While this ground was very defensible, it was also too much ground for the small colonial force to defend. Unlike their prior position at Brooklyn Heights, which was two miles long, Long Island Heights stretched for nine. This was new ground to the Americans and it took time for them to sort out their lines. Their confusion was exacerbated by Washington's decisions to replace Sullivan with another general, Israel Putnam, and to combine the army's regiments into brigades. The decisions could be defended: Putnam was well acquainted with Long Island, and over the long term an army composed of a few brigades would be easier to command than one of sev-

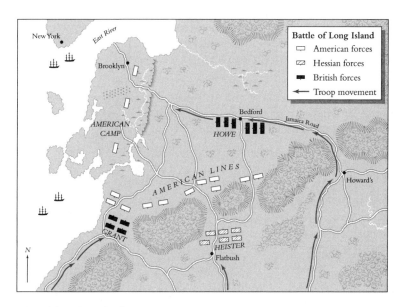

Adapted from britishbattles.com.

eral regiments; but the short-term impact was uncertainty and disorder.

Howe's plan would take advantage of the Americans' troubles on Long Island Heights. He would hold the attention of the American center and right with demonstrations and cannonades while he led a picked force of light infantry, grenadiers, and dragoons around the left of the American position. On the night of August 26, the plan was put in motion as the majority of Howe's troops set out for the pass on Jamaica Road.

Unfortunately for the Continental Army on Long Island Heights, the pass was not covered by pickets or cavalry, so Howe's force went around the American flank undetected. The morning of August 27 found the British poised to attack the American rear in conjunction with a frontal assault by the rest of the British Army. The American troops tried to retreat but being hit from two sides, rapidly folded. While some fought bravely and tried to hold their ground, others fled precipitously. The British and their

Hessian allies eagerly took up pursuit. In many cases they gave no quarter to the Americans, slaughtering many of them despite their pleas to surrender. Washington, who had come over to Long Island from New York the previous night, witnessed the debacle in distress not only at defeat but at the loss of the men and units that had fought so bravely. He was heard to exclaim, "Good God, what brave fellows I must this day lose!"

Safety for the retreating troops was only found when those Americans who could get away reached their fortifications on Brooklyn Heights. Howe chose at this point not to launch a frontal assault on the Americans behind their barricades. Clearly a victory for the British, the battle at Long Island Heights cost the Americans about 2,000 men while the British had fewer than 400 casualties. It was the first in a series of defeats Washington would suffer in the battle for New York.

Despite reaching the safety of the heavily fortified Brooklyn Heights ramparts, Washington's men were still in dire straits. To their front General Howe's military engineers methodically built trenches and small forts to get closer to the American lines and seal them in. To their rear the British Navy patrolled the waters, cutting off any hope of escape. Washington and his men appeared trapped between the twin forces of Britain's army and navy. Yet fate, their own capabilities, and Washington's drive to seize the opportunity presented by Howe's slow approach would intervene to save them.

The effort began in a manner typical of Washington, with a council of war. On August 29 he posed the question of evacuating Brooklyn Heights and retreating over the water to Manhattan. The debate was fiercely two-sided; some argued that as Americans fought well behind walls they should stay and attempt to deal the British a costly defeat. They also pointed out that the crossing would be dangerous because of the distance to be covered by water and the Royal Navy's control of the sea. Other generals said evacuation was the only way to escape total destruction. At the end of the discussion Washington made the decision; evacuation was the plan and it was to begin that very night. There was not a moment to lose.

To prevent the British from learning the plan and catching the Americans as they were abandoning the lines, Washington deliberately did not tell his troops. Instead, they were told to pack up and be prepared to change positions within their lines to relieve other units. Verbal orders were issued to collect every possible boat within the vicinity to provide the transport, and this was carried out with great speed. To row the troops over to Manhattan, Colonel Glover's Marblehead regiment would man the boats. This unit was composed of former Massachusetts fishermen or sailors who were well versed in how to handle boats in open water.

The night march to the boats was difficult; it was dark and the troops were tired. The initial water crossings were in strong tides and high winds. At this point, what Washington would call Providence intervened. The wind died down and the tide reversed, making the water evacuation quicker and easier. Just as important, a very thick fog developed over the American lines, which kept the British from detecting the retreat. Washington himself, after supervising the movement, was the last man to leave, taking the final boat across.

Washington and his army had escaped to fight again. In the end, Washington was able to quietly move 9,000 men out from under the noses of the British. And while the British could claim a major victory on Long Island and force its population to take an oath of allegiance to the Crown, they convinced very few new recruits to join their Tory units. One British officer said, "When the Army was on Staten Island, we were made to expect that as soon as we should land on this Island, many thousand of the Inhabitants would show their loyalty and join the Army. But we have seen very little to induce us to believe that the Inhabitants of this Island are more loyal than others." Part of this reluctance to join up may have been due to the depredations of the Hessian troops. Not only had they refused to give quarter to surrendering Americans but they had also plundered the houses and farms of the citizenry, hardening these colonists' attitude against the British. This view was made clear in peace discussions during a pause in military operations. Howe convened a meeting with a delegation of congressmen that included Ben Franklin, John Adams, and John Rutledge.

Although he had limited powers Howe could offer pardons if the Americans would agree to submit once again to the Crown and Parliament. Despite Howe's recent victory it was an offer heartily refused, with the American delegation stating that the only future relations between Britain and her colonies would be as independent, sovereign states.

Although the American diplomats spoke strongly, the military situation favored the British. The Continental troops were tired and dispirited and had not fought well on Long Island. Many would leave for home in the coming days. Some of the officers were beginning to doubt whether Washington was the right man to be commander-in-chief. And there was still the issue of whether defending New York proper was advisable. General Lee and General Greene advised against it, with Greene writing to Washington, "I give it as my opinion, that a general and speedy retreat is absolutely necessary. . . . I would burn the city and suburbs." Greene saw that the destruction of New York would deprive the British of the facilities they needed as a base to take the rest of New England. A vote in favor of evacuation was made by the generals in a council of war. Washington took what might be considered half measures in implementing the plan, moving the majority of his army north of the city to Harlem but still leaving 5,000 men to guard New York. Hoping to avoid further distress for the populace he did not burn the city but instead evacuated as much of his limited stores of military supplies as possible.

Despite the stress of the recent days Washington took time to review the strategic situation, the political state of affairs, and the military balance of forces. Politically, France was leaning toward helping the American cause, perhaps not outright with troops and naval support but more indirectly through sending arms and allowing American privateers to bring their prizes to her ports. Militarily he knew his troops could not defeat the British in open warfare and that even fighting from entrenchments might not carry the day. He concluded that strategically his best hope was to keep his army intact, using its very existence to keep the flame of the Cause burning while hoping to win a few victories that would induce the French to move beyond military aid to military intervention.

Howe now moved to take the fight to Manhattan. Ignoring General Clinton's advice to land his army north of Washington's Harlem position to trap the Americans in Manhattan, Howe ordered Clinton instead to land just above New York. On September 15 another amphibious operation was put in motion, with British troops landing at Kip's Bay south of Harlem under the cover of Royal Navy broadsides. The American troops facing the assault panicked and fled. Washington, riding to the scene, tried to rally them but with no success. Furious, Washington yelled, "Are these the troops with whom I am to defend America?" Abandoned by his men, Washington remained on the field even as British troops approached. General Greene was of the opinion that Washington was "so vexed at the infamous conduct of his troops that he sought death rather than life." It was only when Washington's aides pulled him to safety that he left the battlefield.

The capture of New York was now a forgone conclusion, and the British would have an important base from which to continue the war. However, they failed again to follow up their victory. General Clinton was too slow in pushing across Manhattan to cut off the retreat of the American contingent in New York, allowing the Continental regiments to escape and move north to join the rest of Washington's army. As the Americans retreated, fires broke out, and eventually roughly 60 percent of the city was destroyed. It is not clear how the fires started, but the British accused the Americans of setting them as they left. Either way, by accident or design, New York suffered the horrors of war.

### More Defeats and the Lessons of Command

Washington was personally at a low point; he could see no path to victory as the situation now stood. Although he had made many improvements in the army, it was still fundamentally based on militia who would come and go depending on the fortunes of war. While they desired to fight for liberty, each man also felt the strong pull of home. Many of the militia units were poorly disciplined and suffered from weak and ineffective leadership. Washington wrote to his cousin Lund Washington, "In confidence, I tell you that I never was in such an unhappy, divided state since I was born." To remedy the situation Washington would write to John Hancock, the leader of the congress, telling him a new system must be implemented, otherwise the army would likely dissolve. Enlistments needed to be extended to three years or the duration of the war, and thus greater inducements were needed to get men to enlist. Washington said these should include an enlistment bounty, uniforms, good pay, and an offer of land and pension after leaving the service. To improve leadership and discipline, Washington wanted to increase the officers' pay, making it higher than that of enlisted men, and to allow officers to use stronger punishments to enforce compliance. Many in the Continental Congress were cool to these entreaties as they feared the threat of a standing army and envisioned a military that mirrored the future republic in which all men were equal. However, the recent defeats around New York and the strong advocacy of John Hancock and John Adams persuaded Congress to support Washington's new system. It would take time for his recommendations to be realized, but at least the idea had been planted. In the interim, Washington would have to fight with what he had.

Washington's army was dug in on Harlem Heights north of the city. As the British Army pushed north a skirmish broke out between the two forces. While the British advanced they sounded their fox hunting horns as an insult to the American troops. However, the Continental units stood their ground and delivered a volley of fire that stopped the British cold. Then they moved to the offensive and attacked, driving the British back. General Howe now tried other methods to destroy the American Army, including amphibious assaults at Throg's Neck and Pell's Point. However, the strongly dug-in American units defeated both of Howe's attempts to get behind Washington's army. To avoid being surrounded on Manhattan, Washington moved his men north to White Plains, taking up a position on the heights behind the Bronx River. Howe decided a frontal assault led by Hessian troops was in order, but that too was crushed with heavy losses.

Although these victories did not make up for the loss of New York, they raised the spirit of the American troops and signaled to the British that the war was far from over.

Although Howe had driven Washington's army off Manhattan and moved his base of operations to New York City, he still had not cleared the island of all American troops. The Continental Army had built a strong fortress called Fort Washington (near the present George Washington Bridge) and manned it with roughly 3,000 men. There had been much debate about abandoning the fortress to save its men from capture; however, General Greene convinced the commander to hang on to the position. Greene felt that in combination with Fort Lee across the Hudson the fort could be effective in preventing the British Navy from moving up the river. Greene also felt that possession of the fort would keep several thousand British troops occupied and with its strong fortifications and artillery could be easily defended. Should abandonment of the position be required, Greene thought the men could be withdrawn by water across the Hudson River. Greene would be proven wrong on all counts.

Howe surrounded Fort Washington with 13,000 men and offered the garrison the opportunity to surrender. That offer was refused by the Americans and Howe launched a four-pronged attack on the fort on November 16. After heavy fighting and a tenacious defense the Americans were compelled to capitulate. Even so, the Hessian troops were so enraged they killed several Americans who had surrendered, only stopping when forced to by British officers. The error in strategy by Greene, approved by Washington, led to the loss of almost 3,000 men and 100 pieces of artillery. It was yet another blow to American morale and would lead many to question Washington's generalship. Washington himself agonized over how the events had occurred, writing in a letter to his brother Augustine, "This is a most unfortunate affair and has given me great mortification ... what adds to my mortification is that the post, after the last ships went past it, was held contrary to my wishes and opinion, as I conceived it to be a hazardous one; but it having been determined on by a full council of general officers, and a resolution of Congress having been received . . . I did not care to give an absolute order for with-drawing the garrison till I could get round and see the situation of things; and then it became too late as the place was invested." In time, the lesson of the Fort Washington debacle would lead the commander to depend less on the war councils for final decisions, but those days were in the future.

Before the fall of the fort Washington had split his small army into several smaller parts. Besides the garrisons of Fort Washington and Fort Lee, he had detached men under General Lee to protect upper New York and had himself moved with 2,000 men over to New Jersey to protect it from British incursion. Indeed Washington had watched the fall of the fort named for him from the New Jersey shore. Now he was in a great predicament, having only a few thousand men to prevent a British incursion into New Jersey. He determined that the best course of action was to abandon Fort Lee and have General Lee's troops recombine with his to form a stronger force. Accordingly, he simultaneously gave orders to General Greene to pull his men and artillery out of Fort Lee and to General Lee to cross the Hudson to join the main army on the New Jersey side. Unfortunately, both subordinates would let him down.

General Greene was slow in complying with Washington's orders, and November 20 found his men still in Fort Lee. To compound this error, a previous night crossing of the Hudson by British troops under General Charles Cornwallis was not discov-ered until ten o'clock that morning. Although the British took Fort Lee that day, Greene was able to escape with most of his men and his light artillery. However, many supplies and the heavy artillery were lost to the advancing British Army. It was another defeat for the Americans.

Now a fighting retreat across northern New Jersey was made by Washington. He was looking for a river behind which he could form a strong defensive line. Meanwhile, at Howe's direction, Cornwallis followed him slowly. Howe's hope was that the Amer-ican Army, suffering from defeats and low morale, would even-tually disintegrate. Howe hoped to end the rebellion in a way that would make reconciliation easier. This strategy was hotly con-tested by General Clinton on Howe's staff, whose view was that the main objective was the destruction of the American Army. He recommended the landing of a force farther down the Hudson behind the Americans to cut off their retreat and destroy them. Instead, Howe sent him on a mission to occupy Rhode Island.

Indeed, Washington's forces were getting smaller as the enlistments of various regiments ended; his army now numbered roughly 2,500 men. However, he had a small core with which to continue the war, and several engagements during the retreat showed the Americans still had fight in them. Washington hoped that with the addition of General Lee's men he would have an opportunity to strike back at the British.

Unfortunately, General Lee resisted the order to link up with Washington. It is likely he preferred an independent command and wanted to avoid joining Washington's army and risking defeat. He also probably hoped that if Washington suffered a few more defeats he himself might supplant him as supreme commander of the American Army.

Washington finally determined to move into Pennsylvania and make his stand behind the Delaware River. Accordingly, in early December his ragtag army crossed the Delaware. To prevent the British from following, he collected all the boats up and down the river for forty miles. General Howe, content with his victories and the occupation of key areas of New York and New Jersey, sent his men into winter quarters across the river from Washington's army.

Washington had reached one of the lowest points of the Revolution. He had been defeated time and again by the British; was leading a bedraggled, poorly disciplined, and ever-dwindling army; and had been ill-served by subordinates. He himself had made several major mistakes that had cost his men and the Cause dearly. There was little in the future that might give him reason to believe his fortunes would change for the better. Yet he would not give up. He would learn from his mistakes, seize an opportunity to deal the British a strong blow, and revive the Revolution. That is the topic of the next chapter. Here, let us see what we can learn as business leaders from Washington's trials.

## Organizing for Success in Business

When Washington was building the American Army he had centuries of previous military organizations from which to learn. However, to a large extent he was building a new type of army, one based on citizen soldiers who were fighting for their own rights and led by men of merit, not just aristocratic blood. And he was building it by combining militia units from various states, each with their own uniforms, regulations, and traditions. Washington sought to build a stronger standing army from these assorted organizations by implementing a standardized drill manual; improving discipline, supply, and sanitation; and reorganizing the army to make it more manageable. He also brought in strong leaders such as Greene, Knox, von Steuben, and Lafayette.

Both business start-ups and existing organizations often face the same issues. One such organization was General Motors (GM); in its early days and in its formative years GM was lucky enough to have Alfred P. Sloan as its leader. Born in 1875 Sloan graduated in only three years from MIT with a degree in engineering. After a short stint with Hyatt Roller Bearing, a ball-bearing manufacturer, Sloan talked his father into buying the failing business. Using his organizational and analytical skills Sloan turned it around in six months. Sloan ran the company profitably for almost two decades, and in time it grew to become a major supplier to the auto industry. At this point (1918) Sloan sold the company to William Durant, the founder of General Motors, and in the process became a GM executive.

General Motors was formed when Durant began acquiring numerous car companies and consolidating them into one organization. Starting with Buick and Olds in 1908 Durant soon added Oakland (soon to be Pontiac) and Cadillac in 1909. He eventually added over twenty companies to GM, which was essentially a holding company of independent firms. Durant's strategy was threefold: to provide a variety of cars for the marketplace, to ensure GM's access to new auto technologies in the fledgling industry, and to integrate parts suppliers with the car manufacturers into one organization. However, all the acquisitions led the organization to overextend, and Durant lost control of the company in 1910, only to regain it in 1916.

Durant was a great entrepreneur but came up short on organizational skills. A major slump in the auto industry put GM into a financial crisis, which led to his forced resignation in 1920. Pierre S. du Pont, GM's new president, recognized that Sloan had the leadership skills GM needed during this time and elevated him within the corporation. Sloan described what the company faced at the time of his ascension in his classic book *My Years with General Motors*. "The automobile market had nearly vanished and with it our income. Most of our plants and those of the industry were shut down. . . . We were loaded with high-priced inventory and commitments at the old inflated price level. We were short of cash. We had a confused product line. There was a lack of control and of any means of control in operations and finance, and a lack of adequate information about anything. In short, there was just about as much crisis, inside and outside, as you could wish for if you liked that sort of thing." In many ways the crisis Sloan faced paralleled that of Washington in terms of being faced with organizational chaos and a threatening environment. Similar to Washington, Sloan also worked hard to reorganize GM so it could meet the threats it faced.

The company was able to move forward by basing its strategy on a document Sloan had written titled *The Organizational Study*. Sloan knew GM needed to have more centralization to bring it out of crisis, yet he wanted the individual units to have the freedom to meet customer needs and grow profitably when the market recovered. Basing his study to a large part on the checks and balances in the U.S. Constitution, Sloan organized GM into semi-autonomous divisions that were free to implement their own business strategies as long as they met their financial commitments to the corporation. To oversee the divisions and create corporate policy and strategy an "Executive Committee" was formed. Financial controls and forecasting methods were implemented to control cash flow and production across the business units, dramatically reducing inventory levels and ensuring cash on hand to pay suppliers and make investments. While these actions seem obvious to us today, Sloan's plan was a first in corporate history. The strategies were also not easy to implement as GM's business units were run as independent companies by "barons" who were highly reluctant to yield any control to headquarters.

After implementing his policies to see GM through its financial crisis, Sloan became president and chairman of the executive committee in 1923. At that time GM had roughly 20 percent of the market while Ford had about half, so Sloan began to implement new strategies for growth. These included many of the activities now taken for granted in the auto industry and business in general. Sloan was an early advocate of market research to drive product development, a novel concept in the early days of autos when many of the new developments were technology driven. Sloan also spent a lot of time on the road talking to dealers to understand how GM could serve them better, stating, "I would meet them in their own places of business and ask them for suggestions and criticisms concerning their relation with the corporation, the character of the product, the corporation's policies, the trend of consumer demand, their view of the future, and many other things of interest in the business." Once home he would implement their suggestions to improve the business.

Sloan also built on the original concept for GM, implementing the idea of "a car for every purse and purpose." To do so he had to rationalize GM's product line by assigning each division a certain type of car to be built for a specific consumer—from Chevrolets for the common man to Cadillacs for the wealthy buyer. But Sloan didn't stop there. He combined the idea of the "annual model" with the used-car trade-in and installment payments to drive demand. He also significantly increased advertising to build interest in GM's car, and in the process the company quickly became the nation's largest advertiser. To help push this approach Sloan brought in a man named Harley Earl, who would become a legend not only in automobile design but in design in general. Like Washington, Sloan had an eye for picking men of talent and promoting them to positions of power.

Suitably born in Hollywood in 1893, Harley Earl studied engineering at Stanford University but after three years dropped out to be a designer in his father's Earl Automobile Works in 1917. The firm built custom cars for Hollywood's elite, and there Earl began to develop his design philosophy. He was discovered by Larry Fisher, the head of Cadillac, and brought to Detroit by Sloan in the late 1920s. Earl's first success was the 1927 LaSalle, which embodied Earl's view that cars needed to move from being boxy and square to being lower and longer. This streamlined approach was a breakthrough design idea that drove the success of the La-Salle. As head of GM's art and color department, Earl was in a position to influence the design of GM's cars and soon began to make his presence felt.

Earl changed the way cars were designed by being the first to use clay models to show what the new car would look like. This significantly reduced costs while allowing more design options to be put on the table. Earl also pioneered the idea of the "dream" or "concept" car. Used by virtually all car companies today, the idea of showing a "car of the future" to excite customers and get their input was novel back in the 1930s. Earl took this idea further in the 1950s with the "Motorama," a large auto show that would take the concept cars to major cities across the United States. These became the precursor to today's auto shows.

Earl used design to drive increased demand for GM cars. Using style changes and new features to both attract buyers and show novelty, Earl helped introduce the idea of the annual model change. He introduced several new features we now take for granted: electric windows, a hidden spare tire, aluminum wheels, chrome, two-tone paint, the four-headlight system, the wrap-around windshield, and tail fins. The fins were inspired by jet planes and were first added to Cadillacs in the late 1940s.

In 1940 Harley Earl became the vice president of design, the first such position in any large company. Sloan recognized the importance of design to GM's overall strategy and wanted to ensure that Earl had the power to implement his ideas. Earl's influence spread to the rest of the industry as competitors hired away his protégés to build their own design departments (by the time he left GM in 1957 the number of GM designers had grown from 50 when he started to 1,100). Beyond the auto industry Earl showed that design and new features were crucial elements in increasing customer demand and satisfaction, and this design philosophy was widely adopted throughout business. By hiring Harley Earl and giving him the freedom to implement his ideas Sloan developed a vital ally in making GM's vision of "a car for every purse and purpose" a reality.

With Sloan in the driver's seat from 1923 to 1956, GM breezed past Ford in market share and expanded its operations around the world to become the globe's largest company. His broader contribution to business was that his ideas became the basic foundation for how to run a large corporation, and they now have been implemented in companies all over the world. Philanthropically Sloan's fortune was used for medical research and to endow the Sloan School of Management at MIT. Dr. Schein, a senior professor at the institution, summed up Sloan's contribution: "His ideas were so clearly correct that we have forgotten that they were an invention."

### Learning from Mistakes in Business

Washington made his share of mistakes: choosing to defend New York when it was in reality indefensible, not protecting his flank on Long Island Heights, and losing Fort Washington and its garrison. Yet after every setback, he returned to fight again. And over time he was learning the art of generalship and how best to use the strengths of the fledgling American Army against his foe. As all business leaders are fallible, they too must learn how to rebound from their mistakes.

One example of a company that did so is South Korea's Samsung Electronics. Part of Samsung Group, which started in 1938 as a small fish and fruit export company, Samsung Electronics was created in 1969 in a joint venture with Sanyo. Starting out as a low-end supplier of electronic components Samsung grew over time to be a manufacturer of low-end TVs, microwaves, and other appliances. However, it lacked a strong brand and in the United States sold its products through large discount chains such as K-Mart and Wal-Mart. It was doing very poorly with these low-margin offerings and was considering retreating from the U.S. market. Then in 1997 the Asian financial markets melted down, creating a major crisis for Samsung. Its new CEO, Jong Yong Yun, had taken over Samsung in 1996, and, like Washington, Yun used the crisis as an opportunity to make major changes. Internally, he cut his work force by 30 percent, reduced Samsung's debt by 33 percent, and eliminated over fifty weak product lines. At the executive level Yun cut perks, tied pay to performance, made each business unit a profit center, and brought non-Koreans to the corporate board. Last, he allowed employees to share in Samsung's increasing profits. While all these made a major difference, it was also what Yun did externally that brought Samsung to leadership in the markets it serves.

Like Washington defending New York and Fort Washington, Samsung's leadership had been fighting its battles in the wrong arena. Recognizing this, Yun decided to abandon the low-end market segments and move upscale to improve profitability. To lead this assault on the high-end electronics marketplace Yun brought in Eric Kim in 1999. Born in Korea but raised and educated in the United States, Kim, formerly of Lotus, became Samsung's executive vice president of marketing. He made a big splash on his first day with a presentation that laid out the company's marketing problems. The other executives were not amused, but CEO Yun told them, "I know what you're thinking. But touch him and you're dead."

Kim's view is that "in the consumer-electronics category, the effective market price difference between a product with a brand and one without a brand is sometimes as high as fifty percent to sixty percent." Knowing that the Samsung brand stood for cheap products from Korea, Kim, with Yun's support, took a number of steps to build the Samsung brand.

It began with the products and a focus on leading-edge, differentiated design. Yun and Kim doubled their design staff to almost 500 people and opened design centers in London, Tokyo, Shanghai, Los Angeles, and San Francisco. Samsung has also utilized top-end design consultants such as IDEO, a design consulting firm, to provide new ideas. Designers are now invited to attend market research focus groups around the world to learn directly from customers about their needs; also, a usability lab to help designers provide easier-to-use products was created in Seoul. Mimicking Sloan's promotion of Harley Earl to vice president of design for GM, the post of chief design officer was created at Samsung, reporting directly to Yun. This provided greater focus for design and enabled designers to have high-level access for their ideas to the heads of the business units. Designers were also given priority in product design over engineers, allowing the outside shape and concept of the product to drive the internal layout— and not the reverse. This strategy has paid off as Samsung has produced premium products with innovative features such as high-end TVs and computer monitors that customers are willing to pay more for. The proof is not only in increased sales. Samsung has won over 100 awards for design around the world, including nineteen of the prestigious Industrial Design Excellence Awards (IDEA) since 2000.

Another major step was consolidating all the advertising from over fifty agencies to one, and then quadrupling the advertising budget. Consolidation not only provided cost efficiencies but, more important, ensured that the brand was communicated consistently across all media types. Simultaneously hundreds of millions of dollars were poured into brand advertising to expose more people to the new and differentiated product lines. Key tactics, such as securing product placement in hit movies like *The Matrix* and becoming an Olympic sponsor, raised the visibility of the Samsung label. To reinforce its new premium brand image Samsung pulled its products out of Wal-Mart in 2001.

By learning that the commodity route had been a mistake and moving to improve its products and brand image, Samsung has moved to leadership. As of 2004 Samsung was the market share leader in TVs, VCRs, and flat-panel screens and surpassed Motorola to become number two in cell phones. Revenues have grown from about $17 billion in 1998 to roughly $52 billion in 2004 while profits have multiplied by over thirty times to about $10 billion. Samsung's brand rank went from number 42 in 2001 to number 21 in 2004, and its brand value has doubled from a little over $6 billion to over $12 (as measured by Interbrand, a leading brand consultancy).

Another business organization that has learned from its mistakes to rebound in the marketplace is the Cadillac division of General Motors. The history of Cadillac began more than 100 years ago, and for decades it was known as the premium luxury car in the United States. To show people you had arrived, you would buy a "Caddy," and the brand itself was synonymous with quality and luxury. However, in the 1980s and 1990s the brand began to lose its luster. Outdated design and poor quality signaled problems that were reflected in declining market share and an aging owner base. New luxury cars from foreign competitors such as Mercedes, BMW, and Lexus were making inroads among younger buyers, and Cadillacs were increasingly seen as an older person's car. Bob Lutz, head of GM North America in 2003, summed up the luxury car's position: "Cadillac was on a road to nowhere. Sales were down, the image was down, and it was saddled with dated styling and poor handling—even poor reliability." Paralleling Washington's movement of his troops from their strong position on Brooklyn Heights to the less defensible one on Long Island Heights, Cadillac executives allowed their brand's strong position to weaken by implementing strategies that cheapened their brand and diminished its equity. And like Washington, who failed to guard his flanks on Long Island Heights, Cadillac's leadership had committed a similar mistake, ignoring its competitors' moves as the German and Japanese luxury car brands moved around Cadillac's position to snatch up younger buyers.

The renaissance of the Cadillac brand began in the late 1980s. The first item that had to be addressed was lack of quality. Implementing an end-to-end quality program and enlisting the help of its unions, Cadillac was able to reduce quality problems up to 71 percent between 1986 and 1990. This enabled Cadillac to improve its warranties from one year or 12,000 miles in 1988 to four years or 50,000 miles by 1990 while decreasing first-year warranty costs by 29 percent. Meanwhile, customer satisfaction rose from 70 percent in 1985 to 86 percent by 1989. The quality improvement focus by Cadillac was recognized in 1990 by the U.S. government's

Malcolm Baldrige National Quality Award, and by 2003 Cadillac had moved to second place in the J. D. Power and Associates Quality study, right behind Lexus.

The next major step on the comeback trail was revamping the Cadillac design. John Smith, head of Cadillac, had a vision of what Cadillac stood for. Smith did not want to break with Cadillac's past design language but to update it. He also wanted it to signal high quality, leading-edge technology and the best styling. Smith gave Wayne Cherry, the lead designer, the charter to update the design. Cherry developed a concept called "Art and Science" to communicate the essence of the Cadillac brand. This design took elements of Cadillac's past design but dramatically updated them, providing a very different look from past Cadillacs and, just as important, the competition. With a shape inspired by the angular shape of the F-117 Stealth fighter plane, the new Cadillacs made a dramatic statement in the marketplace.

One of the first vehicles to represent this design was Cadillac's entry into the sports utility vehicle (SUV) marketplace. The Cadillac Escalade came out in 2002 and supported by $200 million dollars in advertising became an immediate hit. Being featured in music videos also made it appeal to younger buyers, helping to drive Cadillac's age demographics down. Other updated Cadillac models appeared one after another, all with the updated design. Simon Cox, who is responsible for many of Cadillac's concept cars, summed up the new design philosophy: "Design has to divide. Not to the point where you produce a vehicle that really alienates so many people it isn't viable from a business point of view. But you need to make a statement. You need to get people saying, 'I really want this vehicle.' "

Design and quality were two key elements of the reemergence of Cadillac as a luxury car brand. Performance was another essential element. The leaders at Cadillac felt it was not enough for a car to look great; it had to be great. So Cadillac improved their vehicles' speed and handling through rigorous testing on tracks such as the world renowned Nurburgring testing facility in Germany. GM has also replicated the Nurburgring track in

Detroit with the Milford Road Course to enable testing closer to home. Using data from these tests Cadillac engineers have steadily improved performance such that their vehicles now have substance in addition to style. Jim Taylor, Cadillac's general manager in 2005, has this point of view: "You can generate a lot of interest with the look of a car to signal change and freshness but you have to back it up with legitimate hardware. If you don't have no-excuse cars, we wouldn't earn our way back to credibility."

In all, it cost General Motors roughly $4–$5 billion to turn around the Cadillac brand. But those investments in new plants, improved quality, new products, and increased advertising have spawned a revitalized portfolio of leading-edge vehicles that now appeal to younger buyers and command a premium price in the marketplace. Sales, brand perception, and customer satisfaction have rebounded, and in 2005 Cadillac was poised to move beyond its reinforced position in the United States to the luxury markets in Europe and China.

## Summary

As events in eighteenth-century America spiraled from peacetime resistance to full-fledged warfare between Britain and her colonies, Washington was catapulted to the forefront of the struggle for independence. Known for the **integrity** of his character, his **courage**, and his military experience, Washington was unanimously chosen to lead the fledgling American Army.

Faced with the daunting task of creating an army capable of holding its own against the British, Washington put his **organizational skills** to work. At the same time he was fighting the British and their Hessian allies, Washington was implementing measures to improve the fighting ability and logistical system to ensure the army's survival. Despite being hampered by short enlistments and inconsistent support from the congress and the states, Washington was able to make progress in increasing the army's capabilities. In this he was helped by **selecting key subordinates** who could help him achieve his aims. Although he would not always choose well and sometimes his commanders let him down, Washington was beginning to build a core of men he could rely on who would help him achieve victory. Although progress was being made it was by no means linear. Washington suffered several defeats at the hands of the British, and his abilities as commander-in-chief were increasingly called into question. Yet he was determined to **persevere** until victory was achieved. In the next chapter we see how he began the long road from defeat and despair to ultimate triumph.

# 3 ▪ Struggling to Survive

*Seizing Opportunities
and Utilizing Intelligence*

Despite his defeats, Washington successfully executed one of the most difficult operations a general can perform: retreating before the enemy. Although pressed by the British, he was able to maintain his army, supplies, and artillery even as he had to cross numerous rivers that blocked his path. As he was moving his tattered army across the Delaware River to put it between him and the advancing British forces, Washington was to hear more shocking news that first seemed like a major setback to the Revolution but would prove advantageous in the long run.

After the constant urging of Washington to bring his troops to New Jersey to unite the American armies and defend Philadelphia, General Lee had finally begun to move west. By combining his forces, Lee's troops, and those under General Horatio Gates into one army, Washington saw an opportunity to deal the British a strong blow, writing at the time, "A lucky blow in this quarter would be fatal to them and would most certainly raise the spirits of the people, which are quite sunk by our late misfortunes."

Although he was moving in Washington's direction, General Lee did not plan on linking up with the commander. Hoping to win acclaim for himself, Lee planned to strike the British on his own. After the loss of New York and Forts Lee and Washington, General Lee had nothing but contempt for Washington. Writing to an admirer, Lee accused Washington of having "fatal indecision" which was a "greater disqualification than stupidity." Lee hoped that by winning a victory on his own he would move from being second in command to replace Washington as commander-in-chief.

Unfortunately for General Lee, the British had other plans. A patrol of dragoons learned from local Tories that Lee was staying at White's Tavern in Basking Ridge, New Jersey, and that he was not located with the main body of his troops. The unit's commander, Banastre Tarleton, rode quickly to the location and surrounded the building. General Lee's bodyguard, which had given up their posts to warm themselves, was in no position to defend themselves or the general and were quickly dispersed by the dragoons. Lee, still in his night clothing, was told by the women of the house that he could hide under the bed, but to his credit he rejected the offer. It would have been useless anyway, as Tarleton told the tavern's occupants that if the general did not surrender he would set fire to the house, killing all its occupants. Lee gave himself up and was hurried onto a horse still in his robe and slippers. It was an ignominious end for a commander who had only moments before planned to become the supreme commander of the American armies.

The capture of General Lee was perceived as another blow to the Revolution's fortunes as he was widely thought of as America's most experienced commander. Yet this seemingly severe setback ensured Washington's position as the commander-in-chief, which in the long run was the best course the fates of history could have chosen for the future United States. General Lee's capture at this moment removed a disloyal subordinate from the chain of command and freed up his troops to join the main army, proving Washington had that special quality Napoleon would look for in his generals—luck.

Meanwhile, in Philadelphia, the congress, threatened by the proximity of British troops, found it prudent to abandon that city for Baltimore. Before doing so, however, they executed one important act. Understanding the increasingly dire situation, this body granted Washington the power to raise more troops. He promptly used his expanded authority both to recruit and to entice existing soldiers to stay. To exert control through his more trusted and capable subordinates, Washington reorganized the army from regiments to brigades. Last, he increased the amount of his artillery, an arm that would figure highly in the coming battles.

### Seizing Opportunities through Creative Thinking

Although Washington knew the Revolution was on the brink of extinction, he did not lose hope. Having received the reinforcements from Lee's former army and that of General Gates, Washington now had sufficient troops to try to deal that "lucky blow" to the British. As he wrote to John Hancock, "As nothing but necessity obliged me to retire before the Enemy, I conceive it my duty, and it corresponds to my Inclination, to make head against them so long as there shall be the least probability of doing it with propriety." General Howe, following European methods of war, gave a different type of orders to his army in mid-December: "The Approach of Winter putting a stop to any Further Progress the Troops will Immediately march into Quarters and hold themselves in readiness to assemble on the Shortest Notice!" The British and Hessian troops were then stationed in winter quarters throughout New Jersey to protect the newly won territory and encourage colonists to come back to the Crown. The dispersal of the British troops by General Howe provided the opportunity Washington was looking for. He could now take his smaller army to attack one or more of the isolated outposts. Howe, thinking Washington's army all but defeated, did not seriously consider an American attack a possibility, especially as the colonial army would have to cross the partially frozen Delaware River to threaten him. Furthermore, European warfare deemed winter the time when fighting ceased and troops retired to winter quarters. An attack by

Washington would go against convention and have the advantage of surprise.

## Intelligence—a Key to Victory

"There is nothing more necessary than good intelligence to frustrate a designing enemy, & nothing requires greater pains to obtain." So spoke Washington himself on the subject of military intelligence, and intelligence proved critical to his success at Trenton. He had learned this lesson early in his military career when the surprise attack on Braddock's column led to the disaster Washington had seen firsthand. With this hard-earned experience, one of his top priorities was to build a first-class intelligence capability, and through the war he would spend a good portion of his available funds on this critical function. He took responsibility for intelligence gathering and ran that service personally.

Washington had numerous spy networks throughout the war, mostly in major cities under British control such as New York or Philadelphia. He ensured that his cells used proper spy craft for the times, such as invisible ink, codes, and ciphers, and he paid them well for their services. Washington always kept close contact with his spy rings, and information from them went to him alone, directly and quickly. In this way he could use the intelligence while it was still fresh and prevent the British from learning of his spying activities through possible slips by his other officers.

Washington would often mislead the British through the use of misinformation. To make the British believe he had more men then he actually had, he allowed muster lists overstating American troop strength to fall into British hands. He also would parade his soldiers in different villages and have his men build more campfires than necessary to create the impression that he had a large force.

Washington knew that raw intelligence by itself, while useful, required analysis for all the pieces to form a holistic picture of the situation. As he wrote in a letter, "It is by comparing a variety of information, we are frequently enabled to investigate facts, which were so intricate or hidden, that no single clue could have led to the knowledge of them." The comprehensive view he was able to develop put him far ahead of the British. By using spies, analyzing their intelligence, and spreading misinformation, Washington gave his small army a huge advantage against a larger, better trained, and better equipped enemy.

Washington's intelligence before the attack on Trenton revealed that British and Hessian depredations on the people of New Jersey had roused the countryside. These acts of pillage, plunder, and rape had led many colonists to ambush British and Hessian troops traveling between outposts. They also provided a source of information Washington could use to learn of British positions, movements, and readiness.

One of Washington's spies in late 1776 was a man named John Honeyman. At his direction, Honeyman moved to New Brunswick, New Jersey, and became a supplier of cattle to the British Army. He also became friendly with many of the local Loyalists and was so successful in bonding with them that Honeyman was denounced as a Tory himself.

In the winter of 1776 Washington directed Honeyman to report on British activities at Trenton. There the American spy became fast friends with Colonel Johann Rall and the British officers and by doing so learned of their troop placements, fortifications, and camp routines. On December 22, shortly before Washington's assault, Honeyman arranged to be captured by an American patrol and was taken directly to Washington. There, in Washington's presence alone, Honeyman provided the commander-in-chief with everything he knew about Trenton, including maps of the Hessian troop locations and his report of Colonel Rall's disdain for the Americans. After having Honeyman thrown in prison, Washington arranged for his "escape," after which his spy returned to Colonel Rall to tell him that the American troops were in no condition to launch any assaults on Trenton. This combination of intelligence gathering and misinformation was a classic strategy of Washington and gave him an advantage that contributed to his success at Trenton.

After analyzing Honeyman's information, Washington determined that the Hessian outpost at Trenton was vulnerable. The town was not well fortified, and colonial resistance had limited how far Hessian troops could patrol to learn about American movements. The Hessian commander, Colonel Rall, had nothing but contempt for the American troops and felt they were no threat. Warned that the Americans might attack, Rall arrogantly replied, "Let them come.... We will go at them with the bayonet." With this intelligence Washington determined that Trenton was the place he would strike at dawn on the day after Christmas, 1776.

Motivating troops who had sustained several reverses and whose numbers were quickly dwindling was one of the challenges facing Washington if he were to have a chance of launching his assault. In this effort he was assisted by the timely publication of *The American Crisis* by Thomas Paine. Paine was the author of *Common Sense*, a pamphlet many credited with making the case for independence from Britain. He had traveled with the American troops as they had retreated through New Jersey, so he had seen firsthand the condition of the army and the very real possibility it might melt away, taking the Revolution with it. The words Paine wrote in *The American Crisis* were stirring and helped rally many back to the cause at this time of trouble. The first paragraph bears repeating:

> These are the times that try men's souls. The summer soldier and the sunshine patriot will, in this crisis, shrink from the service of their country; but he that stands it now, deserves the love and thanks of man and woman. Tyranny, like hell, is not easily conquered; yet we have this consolation with us, that the harder the conflict, the more glorious the triumph. What we obtain too cheap, we esteem too lightly: it is dearness only that gives every thing its value. Heaven knows how to put a proper price upon its goods; and it would be strange indeed if so celestial an article as freedom should not be highly rated. Britain, with an army to enforce her tyranny, has declared that she has a right (not only to tax) but "to bind us in all cases whatsoever," and if being bound in that manner, is not slavery,

then is there not such a thing as slavery upon earth. Even the expression is impious; for so unlimited a power can belong only to God.

With his troops now reinforced and rallied, Washington drew up a plan. As events would prove, it was overly complex for any army, much less his, to execute. This propensity for intricate battle plans was a bad habit that would plague him for much of the war. The specific plan for Trenton called for three separate columns to cross the Delaware and launch simultaneous attacks on the Hessians from multiple directions. Washington would lead the main column that would attack Trenton from the north. It would be composed of 2,400 men and the bulk of the army's artillery, the men under the command of Generals Sullivan and Greene and the artillery to be led by Knox. While Washington's column attacked Trenton, the second column, let by Brigadier General James Ewing, would be waiting south of the town to capture any Hessians who tried to escape. Finally, the third column under Colonel John Cadwalader was to create a diversion at the village of Bordentown. It was hoped that Cadwalader's actions would prevent any reinforcements from being sent from that Hessian outpost to Trenton.

Providence now played its hand, with bad winter weather moving in just as the operation commenced. Strong winds, freezing temperatures, snow, and sleet would harass the troops as they executed the plan. The Delaware River would also prove a major obstacle. Huge ice jams and strong currents stymied Ewing's and Cadwalader's efforts to cross it. Despite desperate efforts Ewing's troops never made the crossing. While 600 of Cadwalader's force did reach the far shore, his artillery was unable to do so. Faced with this dilemma and believing that if Washington were beaten only his own men would remain to continue the fight, Cadwalader decided to order his men back. Washington had now lost two prongs of his three-pronged attack before the enemy had even been engaged.

Washington's force, unknowingly on its own, continued to struggle toward its objective. At McConkey's Ferry on the

Delaware, the necessary boats had been collected, and they formed a watercraft flotilla of assorted shapes and sizes. Despite their variety they were sufficient. Handled by troops with a seagoing background (again, led by Colonel Glover's Marblehead seamen, the same ones who helped Washington escape from Long Island), the boats brought the men across the river through the ice floes and current. It took all the boatmen's skills to do so as they had to move not only hundreds of men but also horses and heavy artillery over the treacherous water. In the end every man and artillery piece made it across the Delaware.

Despite Washington's success in getting his column across he was still far from achieving his objective of striking a blow against the British. The weather and logistical problems had put him far behind schedule. This meant that Washington's attack, planned to be delivered in the dark just before dawn, would now take place in the light of early morning. While tempted to call off the operation he chose instead to forge ahead, writing later that "I was determined to push on at all Events." His persistence would be rewarded.

The weather soon worsened as it began to snow and sleet. Some of Washington's men dropped out of the march, and more than one froze to death. Although the terrible weather made it more difficult for Washington's men to march the remaining nine miles to Trenton, it did have some salutary effects; the Hessians could not believe an attack would be made in such conditions, so their scouts and travelers failed to discover Washington's column.

As Washington's men approached from the north, their attack on Trenton began to unfold. The town itself was cut off from the outside by small parties of American patrols that set up roadblocks on the roads leading to Trenton. Anyone traveling that evening into and out of the town was detained. Washington's column split into two, with General Nathanael Greene leading the left-most force and General John Sullivan commanding the right. Watches were synchronized so that their attacks would be launched simultaneously. However, another problem soon surfaced: many of the muskets were wet from the snow and would not fire. With limited firepower the Continentals would be at a major disadvantage against the Hessians. Washington did not hesitate, telling

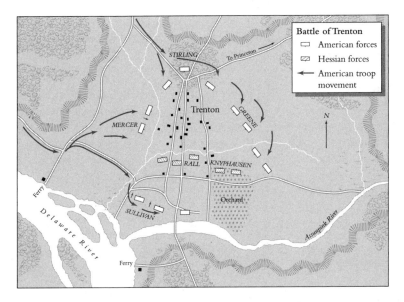

Adapted from britishbattles.com.

his officers that if the men could not shoot then they must be ready to use only their bayonets for the battle. Retreat was not an option; the only choices now were, as the watchword for the operation declared, "Victory or Death."

Washington's men closed in on Trenton, reaching the Hessian outposts a mile outside of the town around 8:00 A.M. As the Americans advanced they took the Hessians' forward positions by surprise. When the mercenaries ran out of their shelter to form up they were met by waves of American troops backed by artillery. Outmanned, outgunned, and in a state of shock, the Hessian sentries were able to fire only a few volleys before being forced to retreat. The Hessian troops within Trenton, hearing the fighting, began to pour out of their quarters. Colonel Rall, wakened from his slumber, began forming his men into their regiments. Disdainful of the American troops, Rall determined to launch a counterattack to push Washington back rather than retreating out of the town. This was an unfortunate decision for the Hessians, as their path to safety, a bridge across Assunpink Creek south of town, was still open.

That escape route was closed when Sullivan's men swept around Trenton to the south to take the bridge and cut off any potential Hessian retreat.

As the infantry on both sides battled it out, the artillery soon came into play. Washington himself helped direct the American cannon fire, despite entreaties by his men to move to safety. Rall brought up two guns to fire on the Continentals, but a rapid attack by the American advance guard captured them and turned them on their previous owners. Now the Hessian infantry began to feel the brunt of the Continental guns. Taking heavy losses, the Hessian regiments fell back and reformed. Rall now sought to take the initiative by moving east of Trenton to attack Washington's left flank. Washington responded quickly by shifting men to meet Rall's move. Seeing that pushing forward would expose his own flank to American cross fire, Rall called off the attack. Instead, the Hessian colonel now decided to advance west back into Trenton to push the Americans there out of the town, ordering his men, "All who are my grenadiers, forward!" But the Continentals had been able to take up positions in houses, dry their muskets, and fire at the Hessians. These troops, plus the American artillery to the north and Sullivan's troops from the south, all poured firepower onto the Hessians from multiple sides.

The fighting now was desperate and often hand-to-hand, as the Americans and Hessians fought over the center of Trenton. In the fray two musket balls hit Colonel Rall simultaneously, and he had to be taken off his horse. The wounds, which would prove mortal, took Rall out of the battle and caused the Hessian troops to falter. Having been exposed to the weather, their muskets were now the ones that would not fire. They began to retreat east of town.

Washington, seeing his opportunity, urged his men on, pressing them to stay on the heels of the Hessians. Surrounded and without their senior commander, the mercenary troops were in a grim situation. When the Americans called out to them to give up, they determined their best course of action was to lower their regimental standards, put down their muskets, and surrender.

South of the town a final Hessian regiment sought to escape but was turned back at the Assunpink Bridge by American fire.

Trapped, they too surrendered. At the conclusion of the battle Washington told one of his officers, "This is a glorious day for our country." Indeed it was. After Washington accepted Colonel Rall's sword as a token of surrender and visited Rall on his deathbed, the battle of Trenton was officially over. The Americans had captured almost 900 Hessians, 6 cannon, 1,000 muskets, 15 enemy standards, and ammunition. Washington's battle losses were minimal: four wounded men.

### Leveraging Market Intelligence in Business

A key to Washington's victories was the importance he placed on solid intelligence and the information infrastructure he set up to ensure that he received it on a timely basis. At Trenton, his use of John Honeyman not only provided Washington with detailed knowledge about his enemy but the opportunity to deceive his opponent as well.

Credible and timely market intelligence is also crucial to business success. In 1997, its own timely competitive intelligence informed the McDonald's executive team that Burger King was going to launch an attack. Armed with this information, Jack Greenberg, head of McDonald's USA, sent an urgent message to McDonald's restaurants across the country. It began, "As you are well aware, beginning in December and continuing through the new year, Burger King will launch a full frontal assault, complete with claims of superiority, on one of our greatest assets—America's Favorite Fries." With this as the rallying cry Greenberg reminded his troops that they had the history and advantage of French fry leadership and that corporate headquarters was putting together a marketing campaign to promote the fries even more. Then he told them how they could help achieve victory, giving specific steps they could take in their restaurants (such as proper fry station staffing, monitoring, and salting) to ensure that McDonald's fries continued to be the best. With the plan of attack communicated, Greenberg ended his memo with reassurance, stating, "If we do this right and keep our eyes on our fries, we will win this battle and make significant headway in the war as well." And indeed, that was the case, as McDonald's was able to repel Burger King's attack on its French fry fortress.

Washington's focus on intelligence was threefold: understanding his enemy, keeping in touch with the mood of the populace, and learning about the terrain he would have to maneuver and fight on. The same is true for market intelligence. It is composed of three areas as well: knowing your competition, understanding the customer, and knowing your industry.

Just as Washington spent time and resources learning about his opponent, Colonel Rall, before he attacked, businesses must do so as well. Yet a late 1990s survey by the Futures Group shows that only 60 percent of the U.S. businesses they surveyed have formal competitive intelligence (CI) functions. So the first step is to put a CI department in place. Competitive intelligence has many uses. The obvious benefit is to understand the capabilities of your competitors and anticipate their actions. However, advanced CI techniques enable companies to see the approach of changes in business, technology, product, or regulations before other companies do. Delving into the operations of competitors and others on the fringes of your industry not only enables you to learn from how other firms run their businesses and improve your own operations. It can also help you avoid missing new competitors that may be encroaching on your industry. For example, the major U.S. news networks (ABC, CBS, and NBC) were focused on taking on one another and missed the threat from cable news led by CNN. Likewise, CNN missed the meteoric rise of Fox News, which won by providing an alternative view of the news to an unsatisfied segment of the marketplace. Following the media thread further, the major TV and print news media have been surprised by the rise of bloggers. These independent writers provide yet another view of the news and often challenge what the "mainstream media" offer the public. Their approach and success threatens the credibility and the financial viability of the traditional media, which has yet to develop a winning response.

Performing useful and actionable competitive intelligence means you need to know not only the basics of what the competition *can* do (e.g., their products, financials, strengths, and weaknesses) but also what they *will* do. When Washington solicited information from John Honeyman he did not stop at inquiring about the facts. He also wanted to know Colonel Rall's attitudes toward and assumptions about the Continental Army. Knowing Rall held his army in deep disregard, Washington could project how Rall would respond to his attack. Therefore, in business as well it is important to learn what the competitors' executives assume about the industry, what their goals are, and the strategies they have put in place to achieve them. Just as Washington knew Rall's mind-set you too must know the mind-set of the competitors. Only in this way will you be able to project what actions they might take in the marketplace or how they might respond to your actions.

Conversely, it is important not to let the competition know your plans; otherwise they will be well prepared to defeat them. Washington went to great pains to keep the British guessing about his next move. Yet too often an executive will lay out all the details of the company strategy in a press interview. Perhaps the thinking is that this will help the stock price; possibly the spokesman simply got carried away while on camera. Either way, disclosure of this kind can damage the firm. The best response I have seen in this regard happened on a sports newscast. A professional fisherman was ahead after two days in a three-day fishing tournament. This was a major contest with a first prize of $200,000. Asked by the sportscaster what his strategy was for the final day the savvy fisherman simply said, "I'll do more of what worked today and less of what didn't work." Enough said.

Creating a strong competitive intelligence function demands commitment at all levels of the business. From a leadership standpoint a CI function requires strong executive sponsorship. Beyond setting up CI departments in corporate and each of its business units, IBM's approach has been to name top business unit executives as "competitive champions." For example, the head of the server group may also be named the "Hewlett-Packard Champion" and have the additional responsibility of developing a game plan to beat H-P. This keeps a competitive focus at the highest levels of the company and ensures that resources can be allocated to competitive initiatives.

At the professional level the CI teams must seek data from all sources inside and outside the company. Outside sources include those such as industry analysts, press, suppliers, customers, and competitor's web sites. Inside sources include the functional areas within the company, salespeople, and top executives. Often the firm's executives will attend industry functions and can provide the CI team with information unavailable elsewhere. These data, along with other pieces of information, then need to be analyzed by the CI team to help them develop a holistic view of the competitive environment and communicate their recommendations for response to the rest of the company quickly and clearly.

One caveat: while Washington used spies to go undercover to collect his information, in business this approach is not only illegal and unethical but it is not really necessary. In today's information-rich environment, most data that need to be collected are readily available. So to protect the integrity of the company (and themselves), executives and CI professionals need to act ethically and legally as they perform their duties. In fact, the Society of Competitive Intelligence Professionals (SCIP), the largest professional organization of its kind, has a code of ethics containing the following principles:

- To continually strive to increase the recognition and respect of the profession.
- To comply with all applicable laws, domestic and international.
- To accurately disclose all relevant information, including one's identity and organization, prior to all interviews.
- To fully respect all requests for confidentiality of information.
- To avoid conflicts of interest in fulfilling one's duties.

- To provide honest and realistic recommendations and conclusions in the execution of one's duties.

- To promote this code of ethics within one's company, with third-party contractors, and within the entire profession.

- To faithfully adhere to and abide by one's company policies, objectives, and guidelines.

This code provides an excellent guide for those who want to perform competitive intelligence effectively and ethically.

Washington did not just focus on the big picture of intelligence; he got down into the minutiae at a tactical level. He understood the positions of enemy troops, which roads would be the most useful for his operations, and what was being written about in newspapers around the colonies. Business leaders too must operate at both levels—the strategic and the tactical. Tom Stemberg, CEO of Staples, makes it a personal practice to visit a competitor's store every week. In this way he keeps up with what the competition is doing where it matters most—the point of sale to the customer. Stemberg says, "I never visited a store where I didn't learn something." This approach comes with a caveat: you need to be careful about what you do with the information. Merely copying what the competition is doing is not the goal. Stemberg recalls when Staples was carrying portrait and picture frames that proved not to be a profitable product line. Yet a competitor saw Staples do this and copied the approach, much to Stemberg's amusement. It is important to remember that simple competitive imitation may be the highest form of flattery but often proves to be the lowest form of strategy!

Washington not only knew his enemy but he also knew what was going on in the minds of his countrymen, the people who would have to buy into the Revolution if it were to be a success. Likewise, in business, understanding the competition is one important facet of market intelligence; understanding the customer, those who will "buy into" your company, is another.

The key to ensuring that your company is satisfying and meeting the current and future needs of your customers as well as attracting prospects is research. This includes formal market research at a macro level as well as individual contact by top executives and company personnel directly with customers. Formal market research enables you to segment customers by their different needs, gain insight into which segments to target, and decide how to best meet the needs of the customers in those segments. The data gained through market research are essential and provide a very rational basis for making decisions. Direct customer contact provides more insights, often at a deeper or different level, because a one-to-one unstructured conversation can be led by the customer. It also holds two other benefits. First, it adds an emotional and personal element that helps drive action. There is nothing like sitting across from a customer and hearing how the shortcomings of your company are hurting its image, or contrarily, what your company is doing right. Second, when customer contact is made by top executives, the rest of the organization sees clearly that understanding the customer is paramount—to the point that the leadership is willing to commit its valuable time to this practice.

JetBlue Chairman David Neeleman is one executive who places a premium on listening to customers. Knowing the drastic increase in the frustration levels of flying, Neeleman defines his business not as an airline but as "the customer service business." To ensure that his company is providing the best, Neeleman personally provides in-flight service to customers on JetBlue flights on a monthly basis. This allows him to talk to about 500 customers each time—and that's where he gets his ideas for improving service, such as adding personal TVs for each seat, unloading luggage quickly (the goal is to take no more than twenty minutes), and not requiring Saturday stays for cheaper flights. And after suffering days of flight cancellations and delays in February 2007 that greatly frustrated passengers, JetBlue's Neeleman responded with a "Customer Bill of Rights" as one key way to regain its leadership in customer satisfaction and industry growth.

The final facet of market intelligence is industry knowledge. Just as Washington needed to know the terrain and environment in which he was fighting, a business needs to know the industry terrain in which it is operating. At a high level a leader should do a PEST analysis, looking at the political, economic, social, and technological trends that now and in the future will impact your industry and key markets. The political analysis includes the stability of the government, taxation rules, employment laws, environmental policy, and regulations specific to the firm's industry. The economic view covers macro economic trends (growth, interest rates, monetary policy, and exchange rates) as well as the micro economic trends in the firm's industry (industry growth, price elasticity, materials costs, etc). Social trend analysis is very crucial today, as controversial topics such as animal rights versus safety testing can create a maze of hot-button issues a business must navigate. Beyond keeping a pulse on these types of topics, more mundane areas such as demographics and aging must be monitored for their impact on the industry. Finally, studying technological trends both inside and outside the industry is essential. Technology advances can impact your company in two ways: new or enhanced products or services that can now be offered by you or the competition as well as process changes that improve delivery or reduce costs.

Professional sports provides several examples of how new technology and processes have changed the playing field. According to *Sports Illustrated,* Tex Schramm, general manager of the Dallas Cowboys from 1960 to 1989, was one of the first to use computers to evaluate players. Amazed by the use of IBM computers in the 1960 Olympics, Schramm hired an IBM computer specialist to design a program to determine which college athletes would make the best football players. Armed with this new technology Schramm was able to select some of the NFL's best players, setting the stage for the Cowboys to move quickly from expansion team to Super Bowl dynasty.

## Summary

Although he and his army had been in dire straits, Washington was able to turn the situation around by **creatively seizing opportunities**. His victory at Trenton showed him at his best.

Washington personally developed and ran his **intelligence network** and used it to study, analyze, and ultimately deceive his Hessian opponent at Trenton. He knew the Hessian deployments and the mind of their commander. Using this knowledge Washington created a bold plan to defeat them and inspired his men to meet the task. Although the plan was overly complex and key pieces of it failed, Washington and his men still carried it out valiantly and gained victory. In the next chapter we will examine how Washington used victories to promote the Revolutionary Cause and help the army persevere through more difficult times.

# 4 ▪ Keeping the Flame Alive
## *Persevering and Promoting*
## *the Cause*

Now Washington had a decision to make—whether to advance further into New Jersey to attack other British outposts, maintain his position in Trenton, or retreat. A council of officers provided advice for all the options, but in the end Washington decided on retreat. The condition of his army after their long march and tough fighting was poor. With strong concentrations of British troops nearby, hundreds of prisoners to guard, and a river to his back, Washington felt his position was precarious. They recrossed the Delaware that afternoon and returned to camp.

Although the failure of the other two prongs to accomplish their mission meant at least 500 Hessians and British dragoons escaped Washington's trap, his bold raid across the Delaware was a great success. As important as the material impact on the enemy, the victory at Trenton proved to be a major propaganda victory. It showed that far from being nearly extinguished, the flame of independence still burned brightly. The victory raised the spirits of Washington's army and patriots throughout the colonies and there was a newfound confidence in Washington's leadership. The effect on the British was just as strong. Recriminations abounded as British politicians and generals debated who was responsible for the Trenton debacle. Washington's action also put the British psychologically back on the defensive, at least for the moment. Colonel Carl von Donop, the Hessian commander, pulled his troops from their scattered outposts and concentrated them in one place for security. Now Washington had to determine the best way to follow up on his success. The answer was short in coming.

Holding another council of war on December 27, Washington laid out the strategic situation to his men. The British had abandoned Trenton and moved back from the Delaware for the time being, and Cadwalader, trying to make up for his inability to help Washington earlier, had led his men across the river to take Burlington. Although the army was exhausted, the opportunity now existed to push the British out of western New Jersey and reclaim it for the Revolution. Washington expertly led the conversation to the point that the council, initially against action, was now in concert in support of another bold move. The decision was made to take the fight to the British again.

On December 29, Washington crossed the Delaware once more and began to concentrate his forces at Trenton. However, he now faced another dilemma. In two days the enlistments of several of the most experienced regiments would expire and the core of Washington's army would dissolve, potentially taking the Cause with it. Washington spoke to his troops to ask them to extend their enlistments six weeks to give him time to deal the British another blow. His entreaties met with little success. So he followed the advice of the Pennsylvania militia officers and sweetened the appeal to patriotism with a ten-dollar bonus. This was met with approval by the troops. Unfortunately, Washington did not have the money readily in hand. Working fast with the chief financier of the Revolution, Robert Morris, Washington was able to come up with the funds to pay his men and retain their services for the coming battles.

Despite the pressing issues of the campaign and recruitment Washington also took the time to issue a general order to his men that forbade the plundering of civilians and ensured the proper treatment of noncombatants as well as prisoners of war. He chose to set a higher standard for his army to live up to than that of the British and their Hessian mercenaries, knowing that this would not only strengthen support for the Cause but also that it was the proper way for an army of freemen to conduct itself.

Last, Washington received one final piece of good news. The congress, awakened to Washington's need for more authority to conduct the war and trusting his leadership, gave him significantly increased powers on December 27. Colonists had long feared vesting too much power to any man and then finding themselves having replaced King George with a homegrown tyrant. So for the congress to grant this authority said they not only trusted Washington militarily but they also had confidence in his integrity. With these matters resolved, Washington prepared his army of 6,500 men to take on the British in battle. They would not keep him waiting long.

Stung by the defeat at Trenton, General Howe moved quickly. He ordered General Cornwallis to forgo returning home and instead take the bulk of the army and attack the Americans. Leaving a portion of his men at Princeton to protect his base, Cornwallis marched to Trenton with 5,500 men on January 2, 1777. By moving quickly Cornwallis hoped to catch Washington's army before they could re-cross the Delaware and escape. Around midday Cornwallis's advance guard ran into an American outpost outside of Trenton. It was led by Colonel Edward Hand and composed of infantry and artillery. After some sharp skirmishing the British pushed Hand's troops back through the town and onto Washington's main line of defense. Despite their success, the fighting delayed the British march, and by evening Cornwallis had brought up only a portion of his army to face the American lines. The rest remained strung out along the road to Princeton.

Washington had drawn his men up on higher ground south of Trenton behind the Assunpink Creek, supported by artillery. On his left was a stone bridge where the creek was quite deep, but on his right it presented a much lesser obstacle. Washington himself rode the lines on his white horse, encouraging his men and ensuring the strength of their positions. He reinforced with artillery

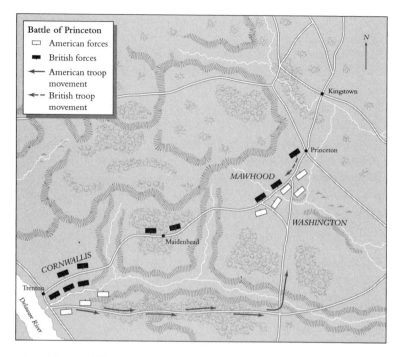

Adapted from britishbattles.com.

those places in the creek that were fordable by the enemy and prepared for the British assault.

With the sun going down and desiring to strike quickly at the Americans and achieve victory, Cornwallis made a number of attacks across the creek with the troops he had on hand. The first was launched at a ford on Washington's left and the next three were attempts to cross the bridge. Despite their strength and acts of extreme bravery, each of the British attacks was repulsed by American musket fire and artillery. The cannon fire especially wreaked havoc on the tight British and Hessian formations, causing huge casualties and stopping the assaults in their tracks. The bridge itself was covered with blood and bodies. Casualty sources are sketchy, but it appears that the British and Hessian forces suffered almost 400 killed, wounded, or captured while the Americans losses numbered roughly fifty.

In spite of his success at repulsing the British, by the evening Washington's position was extremely precarious. With the ice-filled Delaware River at his back he had no chance of easy escape, while to his front was a powerful army led by one of Britain's top generals. Washington knew that if Cornwallis was able to cross the creek in force he could destroy the American Army and the Revolution along with it.

Cornwallis knew this to be the situation as well and planned an early morning assault against the American lines. At a council of war he laid out his plan and most of his officers agreed. However, one of his generals warned him that he needed to finish the job that night, stating, "If you trust those people tonight you will see nothing of them in the morning." Cornwallis, believing Washington was out of options and that a night attack was too risky (especially after a day of hard marching and fighting), chose to stay with his original plan for an attack the next day.

Washington, as was his custom, called a council of war as well. Stating the problem and outlining the situation, Washington asked for their counsel. Some advised retreat, some advised staying to fight. Then one officer, Arthur St. Clair, suggested an offensive option. If the Americans could steal away in the night they could use an old Quaker road to march around the British left and attack Princeton, where the British had left only a small garrison. Once Princeton was taken they could then move on to Brunswick, the main British supply depot, and either destroy it or capture its stores. The discussion continued and more officers fell in behind the Princeton option. Washington, always looking for a means to take the offensive, agreed with this third option. But with morning approaching it had to be executed quickly as well as quietly lest the British hear and hit the Americans as they were moving. If that were to happen Washington's army would be extremely vulnerable and the result would be disaster.

To avoid this possibility Washington ordered a small group of men to build fortifications and start campfires, hoping that the noise of the digging and the sight of the fires would deceive the British pickets. Meanwhile, the rest of the army assembled for the march as quietly as possible. As it was dark and there was need for silence, the entire process took several hours and it was late in the night before the army began its march.

Besides discovery by the British, there was one other obstacle. A warming trend had thawed the roads, making them very muddy. This made marching slow and difficult, and in fact contributed to slowing Cornwallis's approach to Trenton. If the weather stayed warm and the roads remained covered in mud, Washington's advance might be too slow to reach Princeton in time. Washington's luck again intervened. The wind changed to come out of the north and the weather changed with it. Temperatures dropped and the roads quickly hardened, making them much more passable and allowing a better marching speed.

The march was still difficult, given the freezing temperatures, the confusion of moving in darkness, and the exhaustion of the troops. But by daylight Washington had his army within striking distance of Princeton. Meanwhile Cornwallis awoke to find empty positions facing his army at Trenton. The "Old Fox," the nickname the British had given Washington, had not only escaped but now was in a position to threaten the British rear.

For the attack on Princeton Washington again divided his army into two columns, putting the left wing under Greene and the right under Sullivan. Both had a mix of Continental regulars augmented by militia, the regulars there to provide additional backbone to the militia. Now in the daylight both columns moved rapidly toward Princeton. Unknown to the Americans, heading toward them was a strong column of British troops on their way to reinforce Cornwallis at Trenton.

Roughly two miles from Princeton the two forces saw one another. The British column, under command of Colonel Charles Mawhood, had two options. They could either retreat to Princeton to defend the town or attack the American forces. Mawhood, an intelligent British officer who always preferred taking the battle to the enemy, chose to attack, deploying his troops for battle.

General Greene's leftmost column was nearest to Mawhood's roughly 700 men, and he began organizing his troops for battle. The advance guards of both units met with the American infantry winning the initial round, pushing back a smaller force of British dragoons. Then the rest of both armies came on the scene and the fighting intensified. Two opposing lines of infantry formed, each pouring volleys of musket fire into the other. The casualties were high, especially among British officers as the American tactic was to concentrate fire on them. But the tide went in favor of the British when they fixed bayonets and charged the American line. Greene's men, who had no bayonets, were forced to flee. General Mercer, leading the advance guard of the Americans, was surrounded and killed. Other officers tried to rally the troops, but many of them were killed as well. As these troops ran from the field they caused confusion and fear in the new American units that were arriving. Some of those fled as well. However, enough units held to stem the retreat, and soon they were joined by more American brigades, including some who had re-formed after having fled the field only moments before.

At this point Washington arrived on the scene and personally took command of the fighting. Riding his white horse he rallied the men and ordered them to attack the British line, personally leading them to within 100 yards of the enemy. The lines of men continued to blast at one another, yet Washington remained with his men, urging them on. Washington's aide-de-camp found him in the midst of the battle and urged him to leave, but Washington told him, "Away, my dear colonel, and bring up the troops, the day is our own!" Soon the American numbers began to tell, and the tide of battle now turned against the British. Although they fought bravely they could see more American troops arriving and threatening to outflank them. Eventually Mawhood's men broke and fled the field. Washington was heard to yell, "It is a fine fox chase, my boys!"

It was another victory for Washington and the Americans. The British lost 100 men killed and 300 captured, while the American losses numbered fewer than fifty. Washington had duped Cornwallis, avoided the destruction of his army, executed a successful night march, defeated a British column, and taken Princeton. Now Brunswick, the major supply depot of the British, lay open to him. Its capture would be a major blow to the British.

Washington sorely wanted to take Brunswick, but he realized his men were at the end of their tether. The long marches, the hard battles, and the winter weather had taken their toll. They did not have enough strength to march to Brunswick and risk another battle with Cornwallis, who by this time was hastily marching back to protect his supplies. Declaring that "the harassed state of our troops (many of them having had no rest for two nights and a day) and the danger of losing the advantage we had gained by Aiming at too much, Induced me, by the advice of my Officers, to relinquish the attempt," Washington decided to take his army to camp near Morristown. There, the rough terrain would serve as a haven for his men and yet still be a base from which to threaten the British and potentially launch more attacks.

Although Washington was unable to deal a final blow at Brunswick, his accomplishments were significant. His twin strokes at Trenton and Princeton had revived the Revolution, put the British on the defensive in New Jersey, and shown that American troops could stand up to the British Army in open battle. Personally, Washington had won the trust of his troops as well as great popular acclaim, both in America and Europe, for his dual victories. In Britain there was shock and dismay, as Howe's previous successes had pointed toward a quick British victory. Meanwhile, France, a potential ally for the Americans, began to consider the option of providing stronger support for the Revolution. In sum, Washington had been rewarded for his boldness with a change in the war's momentum, bringing the Revolution back from the brink of extinction and putting the British on notice that the war would be neither quick nor easy.

### Promoting the Cause

Beyond winning battles Washington did much else to promote the Revolutionary Cause and make it stronger. At the highest levels he maintained very close relationships with members of the congress and the governors and legislators in each of the states. From his work in Congress and as supreme commander he knew many of them personally and kept up a very busy correspondence with these key leaders, updating them on the state of the army and the importance of their support. He would also meet with them whenever possible, inviting them to his camp or, if the situation allowed, meeting them at their offices. He would flatter them by asking their advice and telling them how wonderful their state's troops were while at the same time influencing them with information and opinions of his own. This would range from discussing the war situation as a whole to offering specific details on how their state could contribute to the war effort and defend itself from the British.

Washington took pains to ensure that he projected the right image of himself to everyone—an image that would inspire confidence and trust in his leadership. The image he wanted to project was that of a gentleman landowner and state legislator who had laid aside his personal needs and risked his own fortune and honor on the Revolution. So he wore well-tailored uniforms that he had personally designed. He used his stature to maximum advantage, always standing straight and sitting upright on horseback, head held high, impressive but not arrogant. He surrounded himself with aides and a large personal bodyguard, all well formed and elegantly uniformed. This stagecraft worked because it communicated reality; Washington strove to be the great man his image suggested.

Washington also had a plan to keep the populace in support of the Revolution, and a critical underpinning was the press. To stay informed of the situation in the individual colonies and Britain, he had friends send him local newspapers. Then to influence the people in these colonies Washington would provide the papers with stories of the army and editorials that supported the Revolution. He also ensured that any reports of British or Hessian plundering were passed along as these enraged the citizens. Newspaper editors, eager for content, would print these pieces and thus disseminate widely what Washington wanted to communicate.

He had other public relations tactics at his disposal as well. The late 1700s were a time of great spirituality and belief in God, and Washington used this to his advantage. As he was a strong believer in Providence, this was no cynical act to mislead a naïve public but a natural outcome of Washington's belief that a loving God intended for men to be free and equal in the eyes of their Creator. Washington set the example by attending church services himself on a regular basis and ordering his men to do the same, hiring army chaplains to perform the rites as well as to counsel those with troubles and to comfort those who were sick. Washington also asked pastors and preachers throughout the colonies to support the Cause in their local ministries with a message that linked the righteousness of the Revolution to the righteousness of God's Word.

## Perseverance in Keeping the Initiative

Despite his successive triumphs at Trenton and Princeton and methods of influencing others, the reality was that Washington's army in Morristown was still in dire straits. A strong British Army still occupied New York and parts of New Jersey, outnumbering Washington's men and, despite the increasing experience of the Continental soldiers, remaining better trained and more effective. And supported by the British Royal Navy, the British Army maintained the initiative, as they could land troops anywhere along the coast they chose, forcing Washington to react to their moves.

In Washington's own army the extended enlistments were due to expire soon, and the militia would return home. Faced with remaining months of harsh winter combined with a lack of food and clothing, many remaining men would desert.

In addition, a smallpox epidemic was spreading through the vicinity. Although Washington was now empowered by the congress to recruit a strong standing army, the difficulties of working through this quixotic body and thirteen individual colonies meant that the remaining winter months would take their toll of American strength.

To ensure that he maintained a strong army Washington took action. Fearing that the smallpox epidemic could kill up to 40 percent of his men, he insisted that all his soldiers have a smallpox inoculation. This was innovative, as it was the first time an entire army had received this type of treatment. The order also faced resistance as some feared that the treatment itself would cause them to catch the disease and die. So Washington had to initiate a mini–public relations campaign to educate and influence the army and Morristown itself that this was the right approach. In the end the results were very successful, with very few deaths from small-pox in the army, certainly many fewer than would have occurred without inoculation.

Ordering shelters built and supplies brought in, Washington did his best to take care of his troops. He would ride out daily to inspect the camp and often would visit with the men, inquiring about the camp's conditions and their welfare, and then trying to ameliorate any deficiencies. Seeing that the free time had led many soldiers to gambling and drinking, Washington outlawed games of chance and other vices. He also put the men to work building a strongpoint that Washington said was important for defending the camp. The men suspected the work was only to keep them busy and nicknamed it "Fort Nonsense," but nonetheless it reduced the mischief. After trying severe punishments to stop the deser-tions (including flogging and death sentences), Washington re-sorted to offering amnesty to those who would return to the ranks. And through it all he continued to lobby the congress and the states for more troops.

Washington's efforts bore fruit. Despite a winter that was actually more severe than what the army would experience at Valley Forge, Washington's attention to and care of his men minimized the losses from disease. As new regiments came into camp during the spring, May of 1777 found Washington's army numbering 9,000 men and in excellent shape for the coming campaign.

### Seizing Opportunities and Persevering in Business

One of Washington's strengths was his ability to persevere during tough times, then find an opportunity to take action to advance the Cause. He did this at Trenton by taking the Hessians by surprise with an assault in terrible weather, thus winning a major victory. He seized a second opportunity when he escaped the British by marching around them to capture their base at Princeton. Washington's ability to win victories, even small ones, allowed him to reverse the downward slide of the Revolution and restore the people's hopes. To succeed in commerce, business leaders need the same talents—the ability to persevere and seize opportunities.

One business leader who has these abilities is Mauricio Botelho, CEO and president of the Brazilian aircraft manufacturer, Embraer. Embraer, or as it was formally known, Empresa Brasileira de Aeronautica S. A., was a state-owned enterprise on the verge of bankruptcy when Botelho was brought in by its new private investors in 1995 to revive the company. The year before Botelho joined the company, Embraer had lost $330 million on revenues of only $250 million. And the company had produced the CBA-123, an airplane that cost millions to develop, yet it hadn't sold a single one.

Botelho seemed an odd choice, as his prior experience was not in airplanes but in large construction and telecommunications projects, such as building Brazil's first nuclear plant. When he was announced as the leader of the failing company, one of the first questions he was asked by a skeptical journalist was, "Don't you think, sir, it would be better for the company if you knew something about aviation?" Yet in a few short years Botelho would bring Embraer back from the dead to make it not only profitable but a leader in a new market, and one of the top four aircraft producers in the world.

Like Washington, Botelho first had to persevere through the bad times, develop a strategy, and change the organization. His first clue to the problems came when he met with the acting CEO before taking the helm and asked him what business Embraer was in. The answer, "Our business is to manufacture aircraft." As the CBA-123 fiasco had proved, the company was engineering-driven, not customer-driven. Botelho set the tone of his future administration by responding, "You are wrong. Your business is not to manufacture aircraft. Your business is to serve your customer." Botelho set about understanding customers' needs and refocusing the company around them. One key learning was that the market for smaller, regional aircraft was growing fast, as commuter airlines were providing flights from smaller cities to large airport hubs. Turbo-prop planes had previously served this function, but they were noisy and outdated. To meet this emerging need Botelho planned to bring out a new fifty-seat regional jetliner, the Embraer ERJ-145, betting the business that the new plane would be the ticket to recovery.

But as Botelho was focusing on the revenue line, he also had to cut expenses. Although Embraer had already made massive job cuts, Botelho knew he had to do more if the company was to survive. When the unions first heard of Botelho's plan they were very resistant to more layoffs. So Botelho met with them to show them his strategy for making Embraer healthy again, promising to hire more people when the company recovered and agreeing to personally take a 10 percent pay cut to match the one he was asking the remaining workers to absorb. By doing so Botelho got the support of the unions and the employees in resuscitating Embraer.

Botelho now had a strategy, a new plane in the works, and the employees behind him. Yet given Brazil's poor economic environment and the company's sad financial state, he lacked the capital to pull off his plan. So he went to his major suppliers and got them to put up the money for the new plane. With this creative approach Botelho eventually got four large partners to provide the needed capital, with the incentive of sharing in future profits.

Botelho's big bet on the ERJ-145 paid off, and it was an immediate success—the first plane delivered in December 1996. Orders came flowing in, and Embraer, which had hoped to sell 400 over the life of the program, would sell 900 by 2005. Within three years of arriving, Botelho had returned the company to profitability and revenue growth, stating that "since the privatization, we have evolved a lot . . . to make us more agile, more aggressive . . . closer to the customer and more effective in satisfying their needs."

To build on that growth Botelho poured 6 percent of revenues into research and development, restructured the company into profit centers, set up customer and supplier advisory councils to provide advice on future strategic direction, and created Embraer's own aeronautical engineering master's degree program to churn out more technical leaders. And Botelho kept pictures of the CBA-123 to remind his engineers of the need to put the customer first. Botelho then seized on a new opportunity: regional jets with more seats.

Talks with customers showed Botelho another need waiting to be filled, as there was a gap between the fifty-seater jets and the bigger 120-seat jets made by Boeing and Airbus. Jets with seventy and ninety seats were much cheaper to operate than the larger jets. Embraer's chief competitor, Canadian company Bombardier, had built a stretch model of their smaller planes to serve this market, but customers complained they were just larger versions of the cramped fifty-seaters. So Embraer went about developing a new design that would still be economical but also be more spacious. It came up with the "double-bubble" design that provided greater head and leg room and put four seats across, so there were no unwanted middle seats. The new planes were christened the Embraer 170 and 190 series, entered production in 2002, and have been a great success.

Botelho is now considering handing over the reins to a successor, but he can look back with pride at what he has accomplished through perseverance and seizing opportunities. By 2005 Embraer had become a R9.1 billion (Brazilian real) company in terms of revenue, returned R709 million in profits, and had a backlog of orders of US$10.4 billion. As important to Botelho, the number of employees has grown from around 5,600 in the mid-1990s to almost 17,000 by 2005. And Embraer has an excellent reputation with its customers, serving as a sterling example to the world of Brazil's technological capabilities.

### Promoting the Cause of the Business

To win his struggle against Great Britain, Washington had to fight on two fronts. He not only had to win on the battlefield; he also had to win the support of the leaders and populace by promoting the Cause and convincing them the war was being won. Businesses also have to promote themselves if they are to be successful in the long run.

The National Football League and professional football have come a long way since 1892, when William (Pudge) Heffelfinger was paid $500 to be the first player to play professionally. In the first half of the 1900s professional football was a distant second to "America's pastime," Major League Baseball. Many early professional football teams tried to leverage the popularity of baseball by giving their teams names that were the same as or similar to those of professional baseball teams, such as the New York Giants, Brooklyn Dodgers, the Chicago Bears (similar to the Chicago Cubs), and the Detroit Lions (similar to the Detroit Tigers). Pro football sought to build credibility and popularity by having its top teams play against and defeat teams made up of strong college players, such as one of former Notre Dame Fighting Irish coached by Knute Rockne. Other ways the NFL increased the appeal of the game was to divide itself into divisions to allow championship games, creating the tradition of the Thanksgiving football game (the first of which was broadcast nationally in 1934) and bringing in top college players to star on their teams. In the latter situation the NFL made a brilliant move by creating a draft that allowed the teams with the worst records to draft first, a step that made teams more equal and games more exciting. This was in direct contrast to baseball, which was dominated by deep-pocket teams in major markets, such as the New York Yankees.

Despite these successes the NFL was still playing second fiddle to baseball when Pete Rozelle was named NFL commissioner in 1960 as a compromise between fractious owners on the twenty-third round of voting. At this time the NFL was being challenged by a new competitor with hefty financial backing, the American Football League. Yet in the end it would be Rozelle's strategic thinking and savvy knack for promotion that would catapult pro football past baseball in the hearts of American sports fans.

Recognizing that the NFL would have more power if he could get the owners working together to maximize profits instead of competing against one another, Rozelle convinced the owners to agree to share roughly equally the proceeds from television, merchandising, sponsorships, and gate receipts. This approach had several positive results. It created "parity," the idea (and reality) that all teams could be financially strong enough to compete well against one another. This in turn increased fan interest in the game. Banding together also enabled the NFL to bargain with the TV networks as a group rather than individually. This increased the money coming into the league from television, and since the networks were putting so much into televising the NFL, they felt inclined to promote it more. Increased coverage of games was another outcome as pro football expanded from just Sundays to weekdays with the introduction of the very popular *Monday Night Football*. Rozelle was able to implement this more monopolistic approach because he'd gone to Washington and secured for the NFL an exception to the Sherman Anti-Trust Act. The exception also allowed Rozelle's coup de grace, the 1966 agreement to merge the NFL and AFL into one league and the creation of the Super Bowl, now the most widely watched television program on earth. (An interesting side note on the Super Bowl: the first title game between the Green Bay Packers and the Kansas City Chiefs in 1967 was not called the "Super Bowl." It was called the "AFL-NFL World Championship Game." The NFL only officially recognized and used the name "Super Bowl" in 1969 for Super Bowl III. The name was created by Lamar Hunt, owner of the Kansas City Chiefs and one of the principal promoters of the AFL-NFL merger. He came up with the idea after watching his daughter play with a popular toy, the Super Ball, and the name was formally adopted after people started referring to the game by his more popular label.)

With these actions pro football surpassed baseball in the 1960s as America's favorite sport, according to opinion polls. New rule changes under Rozelle and his successor Paul Tagliabue made fans even more enamored of the game. These included modifications such as making the scoreboard clock the official timer, allowing two-point attempts after touchdowns, enabling free agency, moving the goal posts to the back of the end zone, the introduction of wild-card teams in the play-offs, and sudden-death overtime. Beyond the game itself the NFL garnered goodwill though its long-lasting charity relationship with the United Way.

---

Rozelle's vision and ability to promote the cause of professional football during his twenty-nine years at the helm of the NFL helped professional football to surge past baseball to become America's true number one pastime, to multiply its revenues and profits, and even to establish American football on other continents. Like Washington, Rozelle had the skills and temperament to achieve this despite having to work with some of the most egotistical and powerful people of the time. In recognition of his achievements Rozelle was named the most powerful person in sports in the twentieth century by *The Sporting News*.

### *Summary*

With his army quickly disappearing, Washington again **persevered**. With the help of Robert Morris and other leaders, he was able to keep enough men together to strike another blow against the British at Princeton. Then, using his organizational skills and ability to **promote the Cause**, Washington rebuilt his army so that it was strong enough for the upcoming campaign. And, as we discuss next, Washington would develop the strategy that would lead to final victory.

# 5 ▪ Breathing Space

*Developing a Winning Strategy*

Washington had been leading the army for almost two years. After analyzing the factors that had led to his recent successes at Trenton and Princeton, two battles in which Washington conserved his strength and then struck the British when he held the advantage, he began to develop a long-term strategy. Realizing that his main army was all that kept the Revolution alive, he knew that to keep the army from being destroyed was more important than to sacrifice it in defending a particular city. As long as the army was in existence, the British could not snuff out the Revolution. However, this did not mean Washington would never engage in battle. His own aggressive nature and the need to show progress to the populace would not allow that. Instead, he would look for occasions when he could take on the British on equal or better terms. Coined the "Fabian Strategy" after the Roman general who had first employed it against Hannibal and the Carthaginians, it would become the guide for Washington's future actions.

As he rebuilt his army at Morristown, he did not surrender the initiative to the British. Instead, he created a number of independent commands and allowed the leaders of these detachments to carry the war to the British. Washington's direction was to avoid major battles but to attack the enemy's dispersed units, harassing them so that the British found themselves always on the defensive and constantly taking losses. Between January and March of 1777 there were numerous small-scale skirmishes throughout New Jersey between the American regulars supported by militia and the British and Hessian forces. In encounter after encounter the Americans inflicted significant casualties on the Crown's forces while suffering relatively few of their own. Despite a lack of formal military education the Americans used speed of march and better skill with their weaponry to win the majority of the conflicts. With each engagement the rebels' confidence and experience increased. Meanwhile, the certainty of the British and Hessian officers in final victory decreased, as did the numbers of their troops. Indeed, the tally of British losses from the battles of Trenton and Princeton and these several skirmishes totaled almost 3,000 men. Combined with losses from sickness and other causes, Howe was left with only 14,000 effective troops, forcing him to urgently request thousands more men to rebuild his strength. When news of this reached London it was another blow to the Crown's confidence that the war could be won quickly and easily. Washington's strategy was beginning to pay off.

### Executing the Strategy in the North

The campaign season began in April 1777 with the British under Cornwallis attempting a series of movements in hope of bringing Washington to battle. However, following his strategy, Washington kept his distance. Failing to draw out Washington and suffering losses from continued attacks by the militia, the British fell back to New York in June, totally evacuating New Jersey and leaving it to the Americans. Wanting to ensure that his part-time soldiers could take care of their personal needs, Washington dismissed the New

Jersey militia so they could return to their fields and harvest their crops.

On the heels of this success came news from the north that a strong British Army under General John Burgoyne was moving south from Canada through Lake Champlain. "Gentleman Johnny" Burgoyne was a lady's man, a gambler, and a playwright who earned the love of his troops because he took good care of them. He had developed a three-pronged plan of attack to end the war. The goal was to isolate New England from the rest of the colonies by taking and holding Lake Champlain and the Hudson River. Burgoyne believed this would make it impossible for the northern colonies to coordinate war efforts with the other states and would also create a safe haven for Tory Loyalists. The execution of the plan involved Burgoyne himself leading one army south to take Fort Ticonderoga on Lake Champlain and ultimately capturing Albany. Meanwhile, another mixed force of Indian warriors from the Six Nations, Tories, and British regulars under Colonel Barry St. Leger would move east through the Mohawk Valley. Last, Howe would attack north up the Hudson. It was this overall plan that Burgoyne sold to the British Cabinet early in 1777. Unfortunately for Burgoyne and the British cause, General Howe had a different strategy for the coming year. He planned to stamp out the Revolution by taking Philadelphia. Despite knowing that the plans of their top generals differed, the British Cabinet did not coordinate the efforts of their armies. In the end this would allow Washington and the Americans to deal the British a major defeat.

Washington, hearing of Burgoyne's movements, knew he had to thwart the British strategy. To do so he dispatched reinforcements to Fort Ticonderoga and sent troops to New York's highlands to intercept the British push up the Hudson. With these dispositions Washington felt confident he could meet any British plan, especially since Fort Ticonderoga was thought to be impregnable. So he was most certainly surprised when he learned on July 7 that Fort Ticonderoga had fallen without a fight.

The American officer in charge at Ticonderoga, General Arthur St. Clair, had taken command in June. He found that instead of being an impregnable fort, Ticonderoga was low on manpower, ammunition, and supplies. With Burgoyne rapidly approaching there was little St. Clair could do to prepare. Early July found the larger British force in Ticonderoga's vicinity.

Among Burgoyne's army were expert artillerymen. Surveying the terrain they saw that nearby Sugar Loaf Hill actually was higher than the elevation of Ticonderoga. Seeing goats on the hill one of them said, "Where a goat can go, a man can go, and where a man can go, he can drag a gun." With much effort the British pulled artillery up Sugar Loaf and prepared for a bombardment. Seeing that the British could now fire shells into Ticonderoga from above and having too weak a force to hold the fort, on July 5 St. Clair elected to abandon it and save his men.

This event was a major setback to Washington and the patriot cause. Because of the aura of impregnability surrounding Fort Ticonderoga and its importance in protecting Lake Champlain, its loss was both a physical and moral blow to the Americans. Many Americans thought treason must have been involved for the fort to fall so easily. Yet Washington refused to be downcast, stating, "I am happy to hear that General St. Clair and his army are not in the hands of the enemy. . . . The evacuation of Ticonderoga and Mount Independence is an event of chagrin. . . . But, notwithstanding things at present have a dark and gloomy aspect, I hope a spirited opposition will check the progress of General Burgoyne's army and that the confidence derived from his success will hurry him into measures that will in their consequences be favorable to us. We should never despair. . . . If new difficulties arise we must only put forth new exertions and proportion our efforts to the exigency of the times." To support his words and seeking to reverse the tide of the Burgoyne's advance, Washington sent one of his trusted lieutenants north to join the American Army, Benedict Arnold.

After he put these orders into effect Washington learned that Howe was loading his men on Royal Navy transports. On July 23, Howe set sail, his objective not Albany but Philadelphia. Washington had to make some decisions. He did not know whether Howe's real objective was to go up the Hudson to link with

Burgoyne, attack New England, move on Philadelphia, or go south to attack Charleston. Despite the threat to his own forces Washington knew he needed to support the troops in the north who were trying to defeat Burgoyne. Moving the majority of his army to Germantown, Pennsylvania, Washington sent Colonel Daniel Morgan with 500 of his hand-picked Virginia sharpshooters to reinforce the American Army facing Burgoyne, believing Morgan's force could play a key role in that campaign. The decisions to send Arnold and Morgan's men would prove critical to the outcome of the northern campaign and indeed the Revolution itself.

With his own eyes on Howe's movements, Washington continued to send directives to the American commander facing Burgoyne in the north, General Horatio Gates. Washington directed Gates to do his best to stop British progress in the wilderness of northern New York, knowing that should Burgoyne be held up the British would quickly begin to run out of food and fodder.

After taking Fort Ticonderoga, Burgoyne's army continued to move south following his original plan. To do so he would have to traverse very hilly and wooded land. This type of terrain would slow an army, but it was especially difficult given all the baggage and accoutrements of Burgoyne's European army, which included not only transport for Burgoyne's mistress but also for servants and helpers of the officers of lower ranks. His task was made harder because the war parties of his Indian allies had attacked and massacred some American settlers, including women and babies, enraging the colonists and sending more men over to the American side. The militiamen streaming into the American camp used their woodland skills to fell trees to create obstructions to Burgoyne's route of march, and farmers destroyed their crops and livestock rather than have them fall into the hands of the British. With slow progress Burgoyne was nearing a town named Saratoga, with his next objective being Albany. Although he had continued his advance and held a militarily strong position he realized his supplies were beginning to dwindle. It was at this time that Burgoyne learned by letter that Howe was not coming north to meet him but instead was intent on taking Philadelphia.

Washington's plan, aided by the blundering of the British, was working.

Events now began to move quickly. St. Leger's force, coming from the west, had laid siege to Fort Stanwix, which protected the Mohawk Valley. At the battle of Oriskany, New York, St. Leger's force ambushed and after a hard fight defeated an American column coming to relieve the post. Despite this success came news that Benedict Arnold was leading another force west to attack St. Leger. Arnold, hoping to fool the enemy, sent ahead word that he was leading a huge army, "as numerous as the leaves on the trees." Hearing this, St. Leger's Indian allies deserted him, severely depleting his force. Faced with bad odds the British officer made the decision to end his siege and withdraw. Although Burgoyne did not know it yet, the second of his three prongs had failed; he was now on his own.

To feed his men, Burgoyne opted to send out a large detachment of 600 men under Hessian colonel Frederick Baum to collect supplies and enlist Tories into his army. A mixed force of Hessian dragoons, light infantry, Canadians, Tories, Indians, and a marching band set out on in mid-August toward the town of Bennington to carry out their mission, with additional instructions to avoid being drawn into a major battle. Things went well at first, and the polyglot unit made good progress. However, Baum learned of approaching American forces and determined the best course of action was to take up a defensive position and request support from General Burgoyne. On August 16, while awaiting word from Burgoyne, Baum was surrounded and attacked by an American militia nearly twice the size of his force. Hit from all sides, Baum's soldiers were quickly overwhelmed, with Baum himself mortally wounded. The relief force sent by Burgoyne was also ambushed and eliminated. It was at this time that Burgoyne learned of St. Leger's retreat. He now faced the choice of retreating north to ensure an uninterrupted supply line or proceeding on to take Albany. He unwisely chose the latter.

Washington, finally learning on August 21 that Howe's objective was indeed Philadelphia, ordered General Sullivan to march north to reinforce Major General Horatio Gates and told New

England's militia to join Gates as well. Gates had by now assembled 12,000 men, half of them regulars, on Bemis Heights, south of Saratoga. Gates had taken the advice of Polish engineer and soldier of fortune Colonel Thaddeus Kosciusko and Benedict Arnold and determined that Bemis Heights was the best place to stop the British. There Arnold and Kosciusko directed the building of fortifications to further strengthen the position.

To continue his movement to Albany, Burgoyne would either have to force Gates off the Heights or go around them and make Gates's position untenable. Thus, on the morning of September 19 Burgoyne sent Brigadier General Simon Fraser with a column of 2,000 men with the mission to go around the left flank of the Americans. Fraser's men would then push east toward the river and roll up the American line. This attack would be supported by one in the center composed of 1,100 men and by another on the British left by a force of the same size.

Benedict Arnold, watching the British movements, told Gates it was critical to send troops to stop it. For three hours Gates refused Arnold's entreaties but eventually relented. Arnold led a force that included Morgan's riflemen that met the British center in a clearing at a place called Freeman's Farm. The British tried to force the Americans back but Arnold took the fight to the British. With Morgan's men targeting British officers and artillerymen and dropping one after another, Arnold's regular troops threatened to break Burgoyne's center. It was only reinforcement by the British left and Gates's refusal to reinforce Arnold that saved Burgoyne's army from destruction.

While the battle was technically a draw, British losses were heavy (almost 600 casualties) while the Americans suffered about 300. Burgoyne again had to decide whether to continue his advance or to fall back on his supply line. Hearing from General Clinton in New York that he would lead an attack northward up the Hudson toward him convinced Burgoyne his operation still had a chance of success. However, while Clinton captured some forts, his force, had it arrived in time, was insufficient to relieve the pressure on Burgoyne. So in early October Burgoyne decided to have another go at Gates's army on Bemis Heights in one final push.

---

The army Burgoyne would throw against the American lines was not the same one he had arrived with. Hungry, weakened by disease, and reduced by desertions, it was also heavily outnumbered by its opponent. And it would not be fighting on the open fields of Europe; instead it would be going up against frontiersmen fighting on their own heavily wooded and hilly ground. Despite these factors and the advice of his generals to fall back, Burgoyne, always the gambler, determined the odds were still in his favor. He ordered a detachment of 1,500 men under General Fraser to execute a "reconnaissance in force" against the American left to probe for weaknesses. On the morning of October 7 it moved out on its mission.

Fraser's men went forward and took up a position on a rise close to the American lines. The rebel army, seeing the threat, struck back hard and fast. The American troops poured fire into the British units and threatened the detachment's flanks. Benedict Arnold, who had been relieved of any command by an envious Gates (Gates had refused to mention Arnold's contributions to success in dispatches to the congress), left his tent and joined the fray. Despite not having any official role, Arnold incited the American troops to press the British hard and led them forward. General Fraser himself was picked off by rebel sharpshooters and fell, mortally wounded. The Americans not only pushed the British troops off the hill but drove their right flank all the way in. Arnold's horse was felled by a musket shot, pinning Arnold under it and breaking his leg, but not before the day was won by the rebels.

With his second attempt to force a passage to Albany in tatters, Burgoyne had no viable option but retreat, and on October 8 he began marching back to Saratoga. However, the American Army would not let him off that easy. Burgoyne's retreat was cut off by the Americans, and with no hope of breaking out he formally surrendered his army on the October 17. With the victory the Americans took prisoner almost 6,000 men, several pieces of field artillery, and 5,000 small arms.

The British defeat at Saratoga not only was a major loss in terms of men and materiel. It was another blow to British prestige and introduced more doubt about final victory to those in power.

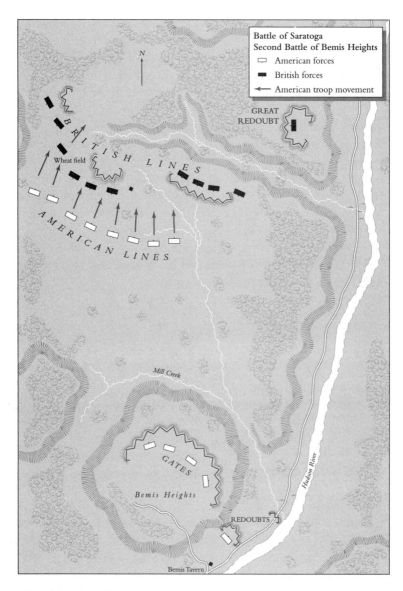

Adapted from britishbattles.com.

More important, it drew France (and ultimately Spain) directly into the war on the side of the Americans.

With a strategy to weaken Britain, her historic enemy, France had already been secretly providing arms and money to the Revolution. However, unsure that the Revolution could be successful, it had been reluctant to take any further steps. The rebel victory at Saratoga erased those fears and would ultimately lead France to send troops and ships to aid the Americans. In addition, it would cause Britain to have to fight a battle on multiple fronts, not just in the colonies. The American success at Saratoga, aided by Washington's decision to send Arnold and Morgan's riflemen, was a major turning point in the war. It was also the first proof that Washington's strategy of keeping his armies intact and fighting the British on his own terms was a formula for success. However, despite the success in the north, problems remained for Washington as he faced Howe near Philadelphia.

## Implementing the Strategy against Howe

General Howe landed his troops at Head of Elk, Maryland, on August 25. Rather than synchronize with Burgoyne, Howe chose as his objective the rebel capital of Philadelphia, where Congress was meeting. His landing covered by the British Navy, Howe slowly moved toward the city. Along the way his troops often plundered the countryside, despite Howe's efforts to stop the behavior with hangings and floggings. As had been the case in New Jersey, this turned the populace against the British and created a stream of recruits for the American Army. Washington, after parading his men through Philadelphia to build the city's morale, had drawn his men up in a defensive line behind Brandywine Creek.

Washington had chosen a strong position, as the creek could be crossed only at a few places, which he covered with troops and artillery. Howe, always preferring to avoid direct assaults on American lines, determined his best course of action was to again outflank the rebels. Replicating his Long Island tactics he ordered Cornwallis on an eighteen-mile march around the American right flank to hit them from behind. Meanwhile he would have General Knyphausen make demonstrations in front of Washington's line to keep the Americans occupied. Howe himself accompanied Cornwallis's flanking column.

Knyphausen did his job well, ordering his troops to march back and forth in front of the American lines and probe them to lead Washington to think this was the main British push. Artillery bombardments added to the effect. Meanwhile, Washington had received reports that there was British movement on his right, but it wasn't clear if this was a major thrust or merely a feint. In the late afternoon it became clear it was the former as Cornwallis's troops hit American troops covering the right flank.

As Cornwallis's blow landed on Washington's right, Knyphausen launched an assault across the Brandywine. Together, these two attacks sent Washington's men reeling, and the Americans retreated hastily toward the town of Chester. The situation was grim for Washington's army. Yet again Howe missed an opportunity to destroy the Americans. Feeling his men were too worn out by the day's events Howe chose not to pursue the rebels. Thus, although he had been out-generalled, Washington was able to re-form his army while it was still between the British and Philadelphia. There Washington ordered more reinforcements to rebuild his army.

Washington now sought to land a blow against the British. To do so he chose one of his fighting generals, "Mad Anthony" Wayne, who had fought bravely in the retreat from the Brandywine. Wayne was given 1,500 men and the mission to harass the British and keep them on the defensive. Moving close to the British lines Wayne felt sure he had the element of surprise on his side and prepared to strike. However, Tory sympathizers had revealed his position to the British. The British commander, General Sir Charles Grey, removed the flintlocks from his men's muskets to ensure no one fired an early round and spoiled the surprise. He told his men they would fight using only their bayonets. With these orders Grey launched a surprise night attack on Wayne's men.

Despite Wayne's having increased the number of his sentries, the British assault succeeded in penetrating the American position.

Disaster struck when Wayne's second-in-command was slow to react and Wayne was unable to restore the situation. Before the night was over 300 Americans were bayoneted. Although Wayne was absolved of responsibility, the "Paoli Massacre" was a major defeat for the Americans, and many raised questions again about Washington's leadership skills.

The questions continued when Howe executed a set of movements that moved Washington out of his position to defend Philadelphia. Washington, concerned about being outflanked again and unsettled by the Paoli defeat, was outmaneuvered, and the route to the rebel capital was open. Howe took it and entered Philadelphia on September 26. Although Howe had captured the colonists' capital, Washington was not dismayed as Howe had not destroyed Washington's army nor had thousands of Loyalists joined his colors in Philadelphia as he had expected.

Washington sought to regain the initiative by seizing another opportunity to strike the British. To defend Philadelphia, Howe dispersed his troops. He garrisoned 3,000 men in the city, sent another thousand to man other defenses, and stationed the remaining 8,000 in Germantown, a few miles from Philadelphia. It was the latter that Washington planned to attack, timing the assault to occur before they had completed fortifying their encampment.

Washington's strategic approach was correct, but his tactical plan again suffered from his penchant for overly complex operations. The main attack on the British would be carried out by two columns in the center. The right-center column was composed of troops under Generals Sullivan and Wayne while the left-center was led by General Greene. Their attacks were to be launched at daybreak after a night march to the British positions. To capture any retreating British trying to escape, two flanking columns would encircle Germantown, one on the American left under Smallwood and one on the right under Armstrong. Another force would make a demonstration by Philadelphia to keep the garrison troops too busy to reinforce those at Germantown. In many ways the plan resembled that at Trenton, but here Washington's luck could not overcome the plan and its implementation and a comparable victory would evade his grasp.

The battle began well enough. At dawn on October 4, 1777, Sullivan's men hit the first line of British. Composed of the elite light infantry the British line fought hard but was eventually driven back into Germantown. Fighting was heavy, and Sullivan used up ammunition at such a prodigious rate that Washington sent a warning to him to conserve it. Pushing the British back out of Germantown the Americans were treated to a nasty surprise. Washington and his commanders learned that a small detachment of about a hundred men from the 40th Foot under Lieutenant Colonel Musgrave had barricaded itself inside Chew House, a stone mansion in the center of town. A hurried council of war ensued in which Washington asked for opinions on the right course of action. Most officers were for surrounding the house to prevent the men there from creating any mischief and then pushing on with the majority of the troops to maintain momentum. However, General Knox, citing the ancient military maxim to "never leave a garrison castle in the rear," won the argument. Washington had his doubts but went along with Knox's plan. So rather than exploit their advantage Sullivan's men encircled Chew House and sought to take it by storm.

Greene's column, which had gotten lost, was now arriving on the battlefield. Although it was early morning a thick mist hung over the battlefield, making the execution of Washington's plan more difficult and increasing the opportunity for confusion. Some of Greene's men ended up fighting at Chew House. Meanwhile, another of his units ran into General Wayne's troops and, mistaking them for British regulars, fired on them. Wayne's men, after suffering these casualties and thinking the firing in their rear at Chew House meant the British had gotten behind them, now retreated. At this time the second line of British troops attacked. Sullivan's men, who had been fighting much of the morning, were now low on ammunition and were forced to retreat. Eventually the entire American attack fell back, Chew House itself was relieved, and the American Army retreated from the battlefield to lick its wounds.

The battle of Germantown had held the promise of victory, but it was a promise not kept. As General Wayne would later write,

"Fortune smiled on us for full three hours... (but) confusion ensued, and we ran away from the arms of victory open to receive us." The battle results were interpreted differently in various quarters. As the American troops had fought well against the British regulars, they themselves were encouraged by the action. And in France the court was impressed with the Americans' aggressiveness. However, others saw the defeat as an added question mark about Washington's ability to lead the colonial armies to victory.

Fighting between the two armies continued on a small scale as Howe secured his supply lines and prepared his defenses of Philadelphia. However, once it was clear that Howe was strongly established in the rebel capital and with winter coming on, Washington chose to move his forces to Valley Forge, Pennsylvania. There Washington could base his army in a highly defensible position while keeping an eye on his British enemy. Events would prove, however, that Washington would need to keep his eyes not only on the British in front of him but also on those behind him who sought his removal, as we shall see in the next chapter.

### Developing and Executing a Successful Strategy in Business

For Washington the measure of his strategy's success would be winning his battles, campaigns, and ultimately, the war. In business the measure of success for a leader's strategy is based on financial results; the company's market value, revenue, profits, and market share. In these measurements few could compare to Roberto Goizueta, Coca-Cola's CEO from 1981 to 1997. Goizueta's strategy and the implementation of it enabled him to increase the value of the company from $4.3 billion when he became CEO to $180 billion when he turned over the reins to his successor. A person buying $1,000 worth of shares of Coca-Cola and reinvesting dividends into more Coke stock would have seen the value increase to $71,000 during Goizueta's tenure. Goizueta also had the distinction of being the first CEO who wasn't the company's founder or the one to take it public to become a billionaire by owning the company's stock.

One hundred shares of Coca-Cola stock and $40 were all Goizueta had in 1960 when he defected from his native Cuba on a vacation to Miami. By that time Goizueta, who had been educated at Yale as a chemical engineer and taught himself English by watching Hollywood movies, had been a Coke employee for six years. After working for Coke in Miami, Goizueta moved to the company's Atlanta headquarters in 1964. Progressing quickly up the corporate ladder through hard work and quick thinking, Goizueta caught the eye of Robert Woodruff, Coca-Cola's CEO since 1923. Woodruff put Goizueta into the president's job in 1980 and then made him CEO and chairman in 1981 with the mandate to reverse the company's downward slide.

Coca-Cola's market share had been falling, and in the late 1970s Pepsi Cola had surpassed Coke in sales in supermarkets. Because the U.S. soft-drink industry was maturing, the company had diversified into non–soft drink industries. This approach had poor results. The company had no central strategy, and several independent fiefdoms had surfaced, each with its own plan. Coke's culture had become overly conservative, stodgy, and risk averse.

Goizueta looked at the market landscape and instead of seeing a bleak winter saw a budding spring. In looking at markets outside the United States he saw huge potential for the growth of Coke and its sister drinks. Inside the United States Goizueta looked at the market a totally different way. Calculating that people drink sixty-four ounces of fluid daily with only twenty-four of those ounces being water, Goizueta saw a big upside for increasing market share, especially since Coke products at that time supplied only a few of those ounces.

That was the market side of the business. Financially, Goizueta vowed to focus not on revenue but on making returns on invested capital much stronger. He said, "I have an absolute fetish for return on capital. That's No. 1 for me. Today, we earn about three times our cost of capital. If you invest in the business at less than your cost of capital, you're liquidating the business." Goizueta, whose primary goal for Coca-Cola was to build wealth for Coke shareholders, always called them "shareowners" to emphasize they owned the company and were the ones management served.

To maximize shareowner wealth, Goizueta was not afraid to experiment. To grow in the United States he introduced Diet Coke to take advantage of the trend toward weight watching. At the time other executives were worried about diluting the Coke brand and didn't want to encroach on the sales of Coca-Cola's primary diet drink, Tab. But Goizueta, who wanted to foster more experimentation in the company and a willingness to take risks, overruled them and brought out the product. Diet Coke proved a success, becoming the leading diet drink in its first year and winning 70 percent of its sales from non-Tab drinkers. Goizueta also updated Coke's tagline from the staid "Have a Coke and a Smile" to "Coke is it!" and poured money into new ad campaigns to make Coke the preferred drink again.

To expand outside the United States Goizueta invested heavily in places such as Japan, the Philippines, China, Germany, and Russia. The expansion called for investments in bottling plants and distribution channels to produce the supply of soft drinks while simultaneously funding advertising and promotions to create awareness and demand.

Goizueta's overseas strategy and its execution were so successful that by the late 1990s Coca-Cola derived two-thirds of its unit sales and over 80 percent of its profits from outside the United States and had achieved nearly 50 percent share worldwide.

Another major move Goizueta took was in his supply chain. Realizing that Coca-Cola's bottlers were not customers but business partners and that many had become complacent, Goizueta developed a far-reaching plan to shake things up. He would strengthen Coke's distribution system by buying up weak bottlers, whipping them into shape, and reselling them to larger and stronger bottlers. In turn, these larger partners would be more capable of supporting Coca-Cola's expansion plans.

Like Washington, Goizueta made his share of mistakes. But like Washington, the Coca-Cola CEO was able to rebound from them and come back even stronger. It was Goizueta who in 1985 was responsible for the introduction of "New Coke" and taking the original Coke off the shelves. Coke, the company's flagship drink, had been losing share, dropping from owning over half the market in the late 1940s to the low twenties by the early 1980s. Pepsi was making inroads on Coke's share, claiming on the basis of its "Pepsi Challenge" taste tests that it tasted better. Hoping to reverse the slow slide of Coca-Cola's market share Goizueta authorized the first change in the formula in almost a century. Goizueta, who wanted new thinking and risk taking, was persuaded by blind-test research that showed New Coke tasted better than the original. What the research didn't factor in was the power of the Coke brand and what it stood for in the hearts and minds of Coca-Cola loyalists. Coke had been a part of American lives for almost 100 years. Kids had grown up with it and drank it on their dates. Coke had gone to war with GIs overseas and was the little bit of home they could bring with them. Families had it with meals at home and at restaurants. Coke was woven into the fabric of Americans' daily lives and in the process had itself become a piece of Americana.

As part of its debut New Coke was heralded as an improvement over the original. Its tagline was "The Best Just Got Better." But if New Coke was launched with a bang, the resulting consumer response was more like a nuclear reaction. Calls to the company skyrocketed, and people started hoarding and stockpiling cases of the original Coke. Protests sprang up, petitions were signed, and lawsuits were even filed.

Goizueta recognized his mistake, and in a few short weeks he and his lieutenants scrambled to return the original Coke to the shelves. To respond to the emotion customers felt for the brand and its ties to their lives it was relabeled "Coca-Cola Classic" and had the tagline "Red, White and You." Although many marketing experts felt Goizueta's introduction of New Coke may have been the dumbest marketing move ever made, he showed his business smarts by quickly reversing himself and leveraging the strong heartfelt links his consumers had with the Coke brand. Free public relations exposure abounded as TV, radio, and print media heralded the reintroduction of the original. The loss of Coke and the resulting firestorm made people realize how important it was as a piece of their lives. Classic Coke sales soared and eventually held a stronger position than before the introduction of New Coke. In the end Goizueta's ability to respond to consumers enabled him to reenergize the brand and turn around its decline. Like Washington, by developing a solid strategy and executing it Goizueta had reversed the fortunes of his company. In the process he made fortunes for Coca-Cola "shareowners." When things didn't go according to plan he quickly adjusted and made lemonade out of lemons. As a result of his strategic thinking and implementation Goizueta set the bar for achieving financial results other CEOs could only dream about.

Reviewing both Washington's and Goizueta's approach to strategy a few key principles can be determined.*

**Strategy is the key to success.** In 1996 a major business periodical had on its cover the headline "Strategic Planning—It's Back!" The article said, "Business strategy is now the single most important management issue . . . and will remain so for the next 5 years." While it's good that this publication recognized the importance of strategy, the fallacy here is that strategy is something that is important one year and irrelevant the next. Strategic thinking and the need for a solid strategy is not a fad that goes in and out of fashion like pet rocks. Strategy always has been and always will be critical to any successful organization. It must be the starting point for all of its actions. Both Washington and Goizueta knew this and used their respective strategies to drive their directives and actions. Without an overarching strategy both men would have failed.

**Smart strategies take into account the realities on the ground and the assets you have at hand.** Washington looked at the strengths and weaknesses of his own army versus his op-

---

*Portions of this section were previously published by the author in his business newsletter.

ponent's to develop his strategy. He knew that as long as his army existed the British could not declare the colonies subdued. He also knew how to use frontier-style fighting when appropriate to defeat the European tactics of the British. Goizueta knew he had some great assets in the Coca-Cola company and that, despite its declining fortunes, the company could exploit growth in the United States and overseas. But he also realized that he had to change the views and culture of top management to see the new opportunities and get them to take the risks necessary to turn the company around.

**Great strategies involve risk taking.** Although he knew he had to protect his army so it would not be destroyed, Washington still sought chances to deal a blow to an unsuspecting enemy. He understood he must do so to keep the British off balance, maintain American popular support, and bring France into the war. Roberto Goizueta knew he had to take risks as well; some, such as Diet Coke, paid off handsomely. Others, such as New Coke, were initially major mistakes. Yet no one was fired at Coca-Cola for the New Coke debacle, as Goizueta realized that blaming someone would send the wrong message to his employees about risk taking.

**Strategy is nothing without implementation.** Both Washington and Goizueta knew that if they didn't communicate their strategy, make significant organizational changes to implement it, and carry out campaigns consistent with the strategy they would not be successful. Yet in business today people too often fall into one of two camps. Some are visionaries who can create great strategies but are incapable of getting the organization to implement them. Others focus solely on operations and tactics, thinking strategies are a waste of time. Both groups look down on the other, with the visionaries thinking the tacticians are shortsighted and the latter believing the visionaries live in ivory towers. In truth, both groups are wrong. Strategy and action are both required for success.

## *Summary*

After reversing his army's fortunes with victories at Trenton and Princeton, Washington took stock of the situation and **developed a winning strategy**. Realizing that by keeping his army in the field he kept the Revolution alive, he knew he must take calculated risks with the British. By reinforcing Gates's army with Morgan's riflemen, Washington thwarted Burgoyne's plan to split the colonies and helped deal the British a major blow. That victory encouraged France to enter the war on the American side. While Washington was not able to defeat Howe's army in the battles around Philadelphia, he was successful in avoiding the destruction of his own army. In the next chapter we will see how Washington built a winning team of leaders that would eventually enable him to achieve independence for the colonies.

# 6 ▪ Fundamentals of Success
## Building a Winning Team

### Washington: Building a Winning Team

Despite Washington's successes at Trenton and Princeton and the solid performance of his army, some in the military and Congress sought his removal. These efforts would come to be known as "the Conway Cabal," although they were less a coordinated conspiracy than a confluence of men coming together with the same goal: replacing Washington.

The motivations of these men were mixed. Some, military men such as Generals Thomas Conway (for whom the conspiracy was later named) and Horatio Gates, were driven by ambition. Others were members of Congress who were either unhappy with the progress of the war and Washington's actions or were concerned that Washington was accumulating too much power and might become a military tyrant. In the former group were Thomas Mifflin, Samuel Adams, Richard Henry Lee, and Benjamin Rush (former member of Congress and army physician);

the latter included John Adams and others. The "conspirators" sought not only Washington's removal but also the elevation of Gates to replace him, based on Gates's success at Saratoga. To advance their cause they circulated an anonymous pamphlet titled *Thoughts of a Freeman* that disparaged Washington's generalship. The booklet also cautioned the populace about their worship of Washington, saying, "The people of America have been guilty of making him their God."

Events moved further when Conway sent a letter to Congress requesting a promotion based on his bravery at Brandywine in September of 1777. Conway was an Irish soldier-of-fortune and had come to the colonies to obtain a commission as a general. Like many foreign officers, he had been recruited by Silas Deane, the colonies' representative in France. The influx of foreign officers to the American army brought a mix of talent; some were excellent and would make a great contribution to the Cause while others were little more than buffoons in colorful uniforms. The commissioning of these officers by Congress created frustration and envy among Washington's American commanders as they saw their promotional path blocked by men who had not endured their privations nor served as long or bravely as they. Conway himself had an overblown perception of his own generalship and never missed an opportunity to praise his own abilities or disparage Washington's to others in the army.

Washington, learning of Conway's promotion request, was concerned that such a promotion was not only unmerited but would also mean that Conway would be promoted ahead of many longer-serving and more deserving officers. Washington had experienced several problems with Congress awarding promotions; these often resulted in bruised feelings among his staff and even resignations. Washington, in addition to viewing Conway's promotion as inequitable and unmerited, could not afford to lose his more experienced generals. Thus he worked to squash it with a letter of his own to Congress, stating, "General Conway's merit as an Officer, and his importance in this Army, exist more in his own imagination than in reality: For it is a maxim with him, to leave no service of his own untold, nor to want any thing which is to be obtained by importunity"; then he added, "It will be impossible for me to be of any further service if such insuperable difficulties are thrown in my way." This last statement gave Washington's enemies in Congress a reason to promote Conway.

In the meantime, Conway was corresponding with others who opposed Washington, including General Gates. In a letter to Gates in late October Conway wrote, "Heaven has been determined to save your country, or a weak General and bad counsellors would have ruined it." Washington found out about this letter and wrote to Conway to let him know he was aware of its contents.

Instead of turning down Conway's promotion request, Washington's enemies in Congress found a way to appoint him inspector general of the army and Gates as president of the war board. These two would oversee Washington's every action and, the thinking was, drive him from service. The cabal now thought it had all the pieces in place to force Washington's retirement. However, when Conway received an icy reception at Valley Forge from Washington and his officers, he resorted again to writing letters, including an angry one to Washington himself. Washington sent the letter to Congress, explaining that while he did not personally care for Conway he provided him all the support he had requested. In the end, Conway's insubordinate letters, a trip by Conway and Gates to Congress in which they tried to cover their actions, and strong support for Washington by his officers and the public led to the collapse of the cabal. In fact, support for Washington grew after the shoddy actions of the cabal's members. Afterward, Gates was sent back to his army and Conway posted to another command elsewhere. He eventually resigned. However, Conway continued to carp about Washington until he was challenged to a duel by General John Cadwalader. Cadwalader, hoping to shut Conway up forever, shot him in the mouth, thus ending his recriminations.

It had been a close call, but Washington's men supported him because they knew his strength of character and his own devotion to the Cause. They also knew Washington sought their counsel, strove to be fair with them, worked hard to help them build a stronger army, and stood by them despite their own mistakes.

Throughout the war Washington relied on a number of key officers to assist him. While his style tended to be very formal, he did develop close relationships with many of his men. Most of the time these officers could be depended on, yet there were times when they either made mistakes or, in the worst case, betrayed him and the Revolution.

Nathanael Greene was one of Washington's most trusted subordinates. The two men respected one another from the start. The infringements of the Crown against the colonies had led Greene to learn all he could about military matters and become the leader of his colony's Continental regiments. Greene was a voracious reader of military history and tactics, and this knowledge set him apart from many contemporaries, such that he became a brigadier general in short order. Although he committed a very costly mistake in recommending to Washington that his namesake fortress be defended, he still continued to be one of the officers Washington relied on as a sounding board as well as a subordinate commander of troops in several battles. In fact, Washington told Congress that should he be killed in action, Greene should be elevated to replace him.

Knowing Greene had not only leadership capabilities but organizational ones as well, Washington made him quartermaster general while the army was at Valley Forge. During the next year, Greene would reorganize the existing supply and logistics confusion into a system that enabled Washington's army to move much more quickly while maintaining a somewhat steady flow of resources to keep it in action. Washington had such a high opinion of Greene that when the war moved south and General Gates suffered a huge defeat at the hands of the British, he recommended Greene to replace Gates. It is to Washington's credit that he willingly let Greene go from his side to an independent command where he could have the most positive influence on the war.

Henry Knox was another leader who had learned military strategy from books and became indispensable to Washington early in the war. Knox was instrumental in forcing the British from Boston when he brought the artillery from Fort Ticonderoga to help besiege the occupied city. On the other hand, he would let

Washington down in the battle of Germantown when he recommended that Chew House be taken instead of continuing to put pressure on the rest of the British Army. Yet Knox more than atoned for that mistake by making the artillery a strong asset for the Continental Army. He trained raw recruits in the complexities of gunnery, created a strong esprit de corps among his men, built foundries to produce cannon in the colonies, and challenged the current military wisdom by using artillery in a more mobile fashion and more frequently than had been the custom in European wars. Knox used his new strategy at Trenton and Princeton with excellent results, providing the American infantry with close fire support that played havoc with the enemy while improving the morale of the Continentals.

Like many other American officers, Knox was threatened with replacement by a foreign officer sent by Silas Deane in France. General Philippe du Coudray came armed with a "contract" from Deane and announced himself head of the army's artillery. Washington, knowing a takeover by du Coudray would likely cause him to lose Knox, wrote to Congress in support of his subordinate. "General Knox, who has deservedly acquired the character of one of the most valuable officers in the service, and who combating almost innumerable difficulties in the department he fills has placed the artillery upon a footing that does him the greatest honor; he, I am persuaded, would consider himself injured by an appointment superseding his command, and would not think himself at liberty to continue in the service. Should such an event take place in the present state of things, there would be too much reason to apprehend a train of ills, such as might confuse and unhinge this important department." With Washington's support, Knox retained his command and du Coudray helped the situation by falling into a river with his horse and drowning. Washington's loyalty to Knox would be repaid later at the siege of Yorktown, when Knox's guns and tactics helped force the surrender of the British.

Although many foreign officers, such as Thomas Conway, merely created headaches for Washington, there were some who in Washington's opinion were critical to the success of the army. The Marquis de Lafayette was such an officer.

Lafayette came from a line of minor nobility who had served France well in its wars. They had also amassed a large fortune. Lafayette's father was killed when the boy was only two years old, while fighting against the British at the Battle of Minden. Lafayette joined the French army at a young age and loved the military life; however, reforms in the military led him to be side-lined in the reserves with little chance of promotion. Interested in military affairs, he watched as the Americans battled France's ancient enemy and saw an opportunity for service and glory. Meeting with Silas Deane in late 1776, Lafayette requested a major general's commission and offered to serve without pay, taking only expenses. Deane accepted his offer, and the nineteen-year-old Lafayette arrived in the colonies in June 1777.

While Washington was frustrated and tired of the long line of foreign officers being sent his way, Lafayette's personality and earnestness won him over. In time the relationship between the older Washington and the young Frenchman would become much like that of a father and son, with Washington in fact telling Lafayette he should consider the commander-in-chief as "father and friend." While he could not immediately give Lafayette a combat command, Washington made him part of his council of advisors, and Lafayette's popularity grew not only with the inner circle of officers but the entire army.

Lafayette's first chance for glory came at the Battle of Brandywine. As Cornwallis's flanking movement pushed back the American left, Lafayette entered the fray to rally Conway's brigade. He performed valiantly until he was shot in the leg, but his efforts helped stall the British attack until the rest of the American army could retreat. After his recovery in November 1777, Washington gave Lafayette command of a small, 300-man detachment, with the mission of learning British intentions. After a skirmish with and defeat of the Hessian forces, the Frenchman earned the right to command a division of the army.

Lafayette proved to be an excellent commander. To overcome his youth and lack of experience, he studied the art of warfare incessantly and always sought to listen more than speak. He took great care for the welfare of his men, at times paying for their uniforms and supplies from his own pocket. Lafayette also served the Cause by cementing the ties between France and the colonies, at one time returning to France to help strengthen the French commitment.

Militarily, Lafayette's biggest contribution came in the final moves leading to the siege at Yorktown. At first evading Cornwallis, he soon turned on him after being reinforced and helped maneuver the British general into falling back to that town. Once the British had occupied Yorktown, Lafayette prevented them from leaving by sealing off all avenues of escape. Washington was clearly right in seeing Lafayette as a leader of men and offering him independent commands.

While Washington was for the most part an excellent judge of character, even he could be fooled. Benedict Arnold, whose name is synonymous with "traitor" to Americans, actually contributed significantly to the Cause before he betrayed both it and Washington.

Arnold played a major role at the Battle of Saratoga, an important victory for the fledgling country. Prior to that he had helped in the capture of Fort Ticonderoga and was nominated by Washington to lead an attack on Canada. The campaign ultimately failed, but Arnold's leadership was instrumental in its early successes and in holding the small American force together as it retreated through the wilderness. Later, to check a British move down Lake Champlain, Arnold got Washington's permission to build a makeshift navy to stop them. After constructing the flotilla from scratch he led it against the larger British fleet. Although tactically defeated in a savage battle lasting seven hours, Arnold won a strategic victory by stalling the British long enough that it was too late in the season for them to advance. The British retreat to Canada relieved pressure on Washington, who at the time was fighting rear guard actions in New York.

Despite his successes, Arnold had been accused by officers of mismanagement of funds, leading to a court-martial. He had also been passed over for promotion by Congress. While the promotion eventually came with Washington's help, Arnold was still denied seniority over those promoted ahead of him; he was so embittered that he resigned his commission in the middle of 1777. Although he returned for service in time for the Saratoga campaign, even there Arnold ran into difficulties, being relieved of his command by General Gates over disagreements in strategy and conflicts in personality. His leadership was critical to victory in that campaign, but he also suffered a leg wound that left him severely crippled.

As reward for his service, Washington gave Arnold command of Philadelphia after the British had evacuated the city. There Arnold made two mistakes: he married Peggy Shippen, the beautiful daughter of a leading Tory family, and he engaged in a number of financial schemes and high-profile entertaining that left him in debt and open to criticism. After another court-martial, Arnold was found guilty on two charges and received a reprimand from Washington.

By this time, Arnold had already made overtures to the British to turn traitor, his motivations being the slights he had received in the American Army, the hope of financial gain, and the urgings of his Tory wife. To increase his value to the British, Arnold sought command of the key post of West Point. With it under his command, he planned to turn it over to the British for the sum of 10,000 pounds and a commission in the British Army. Arnold's perfidious plan came close to fruition but was discovered by the capture of Arnold's British contact, Major John André. Learning of André's capture, he escaped on the British warship *Vulture*. Coincidentally, Washington was coming that very day to meet with Arnold and so learned of his treachery almost immediately. Dismayed by Arnold's actions, Washington nonetheless moved quickly to secure West Point and the plot failed. Arnold went on to serve in minor actions for the British Army but was never given a major command.

Although Washington didn't foresee Arnold's treason and made other errors of judgment with his subordinates, on the whole he exercised effective leadership. In most cases he selected the right officers, delegated major responsibilities to them, and sought their advice. Although councils of war had been used often by generals, Washington used them very extensively. Most of his major decisions were made only after he had consulted his officers in a war council. Although this approach was slow and sometimes produced poor advice, it had many benefits. It allowed Washington to get many points of view from his subordinates and listen to strong debates over the right course of action. The councils also strengthened the commitment of Washington's officers, as they valued being allowed to argue their point of view. Later in the war, as Washington gained more experience and confidence in his own thinking and instincts, he changed the purpose of the councils. From being meetings to produce a general consensus that would lead to a course of action, they became a forum for debate after which Washington made the final decision. In this way he retained the positives of war councils while mitigating their tendency toward group-think or indecision.

### Valley Forge: Fixing Major Organizational Problems

Washington selected Valley Forge for his winter encampment because it put the American Army in a position to protect key parts of Pennsylvania and monitor British movements. It was in hilly territory so it could be easily defended. The surrounding area was rich and fertile enough to support the army as well. From these vantage points Valley Forge was a solid choice.

Yet for Americans the words "Valley Forge" conjure images of ragged and barefooted soldiers shivering around campfires while the snow swirls and mounts around them. And that was indeed the reality. One commander wrote to his governor that "with respect to clothing, near one half of them [are] destitute of any kind of shoes or stockings to their feet, and I may add many without either Breeches shirts or blankets exposed as they are unavoidably obliged to be to all the inclemencies of the cold season living in log huts without doors or floors." A private soldier wrote, "We were absolutely, literally starved. . . . I did not put a single morsel of victuals into my mouth for four days and as many nights, except a little black birch bark which I gnawed off a stick of wood."

Because of a broken logistical system Washington's army would have great difficulty in procuring sufficient food and clothing to last them through the winter. Although the winter was milder than the one the army had suffered through at Morristown, it was harsh enough given the lack of adequate clothes and food. Compounding the shortfalls of supplies were disease caused by cramped quarters and limited medical provisions. Illnesses such as dysentery, pneumonia, and typhus sickened and killed many; Washington lost 2,000 men that winter. And at any one time another 4,000 might be ill and unable to function. On the subject of provisions and logistics, Washington wrote the president of Congress, Henry Laurens, that "unless more vigorous exertions and better regulations take place in that line and immediately, This Army must dissolve."

Despite Washington's entreaties to Congress and the states, little help was forthcoming initially. So it was at this juncture that Washington appointed Nathanael Greene as quartermaster general, with the mandate to fix the supply system. Greene was not interested in the job, as he felt there was little glory and honor to be had in arranging for troops to be fed and clothed. However, he accepted despite his reservations and set about reorganizing the army's logistical structure. He was forced to commandeer supplies from the local populace, since many of them preferred hard British gold to the wildly inflated Continental money. This did not create a steady stream of arms, ammunition, food, and uniforms flowing into the American encampment, but it did improve the situation significantly. Greene was helped by the fortuitous capture of British supplies and increased aid by France, which formally entered the war as an ally in 1778.

The other critical action Washington took was in training the army. It had improved since the beginning of the war, but it still lacked a common drill manual, with different units following either the British, French, or Prussian style. The Americans had enjoyed great success using the frontier fighting approach at battles such as Lexington, Concord, and Saratoga. However, the ability to mass firepower through the coordinated movement of large bodies of troops was still the basis for winning the large battles that would ultimately decide the war. Currently it took the army too long to form battles lines and execute basic maneuvers, leaving it at a severe disadvantage against its British and Hessian opponents.

Washington addressed this by giving responsibility for training to Baron Friedrich Wilhelm von Steuben, a former officer in the Prussian Army who had served on the staff of Frederick the Great. Prussian officers came with excellent credentials, as the Prussian Army was well-known for its military discipline and prowess.

At the time of the Revolutionary War, von Steuben had been downsized out of Prussian military service and had become a soldier of fortune. Deeply in debt due to bad luck at the gaming tables and seeking to reverse his circumstances, von Steuben sought service with the American Army. He met with Washington in February of 1778, and Washington, knowledgeable of von Steuben's experience, gave him the task of developing a training manual and program for the army.

Rather than immediately impose a full-fledged Prussian or other European approach on the American Army, von Steuben took time to learn about the soldiers with whom he was dealing. He quickly found the American soldier to be quite different from soldiers in Europe. In a letter to a friend, von Steuben wrote that while in Europe an officer could tell a soldier, " 'Do this,' and he doeth it; but I am obliged to say, 'This is the reason why you ought to do that'; and then he does it."

When communicating with his men von Steuben faced an additional hurdle; he did not speak English very well. So von Steuben would speak or give commands in French and an American officer would translate—even when the Prussian would swear at his men to get them motivated or punctuate a point. He might also throw in one of the few English words he did know, "Goddamn." Von Steuben's willingness to train the men himself day in and day out, his understanding of their needs and motivations, and his winning personality all combined to make him a favorite of the troops. They responded to his teaching methods and the new drill manual he put in place and soon became much more proficient as soldiers.

One novel method von Steuben employed was to "train the trainers." He focused on training a "model company" of 100 men and then used them to help him train the other troops. Von Steuben also saw to it that raw recruits were trained in a "school" to learn the rudiments of soldiering before they joined their unit. This way every soldier coming into the army had the same level of training and the battle units did not have to spend time teaching new recruits. Last, von Steuben went beyond training troops to develop an improved camp layout and sanitation system. This helped reduce the sickness that plagued the army and made it healthy for the coming battles in 1778. Despite the hardships of the winter, through the efforts of Washington, Greene, and von Steuben the army that left Valley Forge was tougher, better trained, and more effective than the one that had entered it a few months before.

### Building a Winning Team in Business

It took Washington a long time to develop a group of leaders who would eventually help him win the war. And in the process he had to suffer many fools as well as others who betrayed him. In business it takes time, insight into people, and a willingness to try new methods and approaches to create a winning team.

In the realm of sports and particularly Major League Baseball, probably no one is more successful at selecting winners than the general manager of the Oakland A's, Billy Beane. The celebrated subject of Michael Lewis's best-selling book *Moneyball*, Beane has become legendary for his ability to consistently find great players for much less money than his wealthier opponents. Despite having a budget only a third of the size of the biggest spender in baseball (the Yankees) to attract major league players, Billy Beane was able to get to the play-offs and play competitively more often than was expected. In fact, in the five years prior to 2003, the win-loss record of Beane's team was second to the Yankees even though the team had only the eighteenth-largest budget in baseball.

What was Beane's secret? The existing way of selecting talent, the "tried and true" method, was to use retired ballplayers as scouts to find promising young high school players; Beane saw this as unscientific and a huge waste of money. Signing bonuses and salaries had become so big that making a mistake could cost a club millions of dollars and lost opportunities to win pennants. Yet that was how it was done in Major League Baseball, a multibillion-dollar business.

Beane saw a better way: statistics. Rather than having recruits come up and do some wind sprints and batting over a few days at tryouts, Beane would look at how well potential players had performed over a number of seasons. Instead of recruiting from high school players, who tended to be less mature and played against teams of wildly varying capabilities, Beane looked at college players who had more playing time against higher-quality teams. To do a statistical analysis of their performance, Beane brought in a Harvard graduate, Paul DePodesta. Paul had never played major league ball, but he had a personal computer filled with information on players. And he also looked at the statistics in new ways; he determined that the old metrics such as RBIs were less valuable as indicators of success than new ones, such as on-base percentage and total bases. This too went against the grain of baseball logic.

Obviously, the new method of selecting players didn't go down well with Beane's older scouts. It was something new, it was being done by a kid who had never played ball, it was against tradition—and it threatened their jobs. But Beane persevered, and his record for selecting talent, winning games, and making it to the play-offs proved him right. Now most major league teams follow his lead, for to stay with the old ways is to court failure. But because Beane's philosophy and strategic approach drive not only recruiting but also the Oakland A's player trades, minor league system, and in-game strategy, they are hard to replicate.

What does Beane's approach have to do with Washington and business? Washington, the innovator who was always looking for new approaches, would likely have smiled upon Beane's philosophy. And modern business can certainly use a more scientific approach to hiring employees. Frankly, today's method of hiring people has not advanced much since Washington's time. Most companies rely on school grades for new hires and references for professional hires in addition to one-hour in-person interviews. Even hiring CEOs, although it takes longer, is not a very robust process, as is shown by how many CEOs fail to deliver on their expectations.

Some new methods are emerging. Psychological tests that discern fit with the company culture as well as other insights are being used more frequently. Other tests, such as the Test of Attentional and Interpersonal Style (TAIS) and Meyers-Briggs, allow employers to help current workers understand their work style and improve team cooperation and output. Alpine Confections learned from TAIS that one reason it was not moving quickly enough in the marketplace was that its people were better at thinking than they were at doing. Other hiring consultants provide simulations that test how candidates would deal with a real-life situation. A company called Development Dimensions International (DDI) runs full-day simulations that immerse the candidate in a number of scenarios that test his or her capabilities. The simulation can focus on the financial area, personnel, marketing, or operations—or a combination of all. And it is videotaped so the people doing the analysis can see everything. This type of testing may seem like a major investment of time and money, but it helps companies get employees who will make a long-term contribution rather than just take up space or cause disruption.

Getting the right people on board and developing the right team is only the beginning. Washington not only had to build trust between himself and officers from other colonies; he also had to get every soldier in the army to trust in him and their other leaders. He did so by always acting with integrity, treating them fairly, looking out for their welfare, communicating to them regularly, and working hard to improve his own skills as a general.

In business, trust is essential as well. Creating a sense of trust both between the highest officers in the company and between them and all the employees is difficult but must be accomplished if a company is to maximize its opportunity for success. *Fortune* magazine uses an approach based on extensive research by Robert Levering to determine the level of trust a company has. The companies that rank at the top are considered the best to work for. Comparing the financial returns from the top 100 companies against Standard and Poor's (S&P) 500 portfolio from 1997–2004 showed that the best companies to work for would provide five times the return of the S&P 500.

What characterizes these top companies? Levering believes several traits are key to trust. One is credibility; do the employees believe what their leaders are saying and will those leaders follow through on their commitments? Do the leaders know what they are doing and are they capable of making the firm successful? Do the leaders have integrity to do what is right? Do the leaders share important information with workers and answer tough questions from them?

Another trait Levering identified is that employees believe their leaders care for them and they show it. Do the leaders respect employees and treat them fairly? Financial recognition, daily conversations, and helping people during times of trouble are some powerful ways leaders show concern.

How proud employees are to work at their company and how much they enjoy each other (camaraderie) are other traits of top companies. Are employees proud to tell others where they work? Do opportunities exist for employees to get together and celebrate wins? Is there real fun in the workplace?

As the numbers show, better treatment of employees and trust at all levels attract top people and lead to better employee morale, better customer service, greater empowerment, and higher productivity.

Decision making and delegation are crucial elements of working with subordinates. Washington's style of decision making was very inclusive and in many ways ahead of its time. His councils of war showed that he valued his men's opinions, yet the councils did not lead to inaction and dallying but to concrete decisions and courses of action. Washington was also not afraid to delegate major operations to his officers as part of his plans. He knew he could not control everything himself and so sought out the best men possible and gave them great responsibilities, both in battle and when the army was resting and refitting.

Washington and his men had to make tough decisions quickly. And they had to do so when their Cause was in danger of being extinguished or when they themselves were in personal danger, tired, cold, and hungry. Yet they were able to do so. As business-people we are often under great pressures as well, but that does not give us the excuse to avoid making decisions. Leadership guru Ram Charan lists in his *Harvard Business Review* classic *Conquering the Culture of Indecision* four ways that leaders go awry in decision making.

The first is what Charan calls "the Dangling Dialogue." Meetings do not end with agreement on the decisions made and next steps, so each person is allowed to leave with his or her own view of what occurred and act accordingly. The way to address this is to close the meeting with a summary of what was agreed on and follow up with a written note stating the key decisions.

Another way leaders fail to decide is by having "Information Clogs." All the information needed to make a decision does not surface until after the meeting concludes. The new information allows people to revisit the decisions made and reopens the entire subject for discussion again. The way to solve this problem is by ensuring that the right people are attending the meeting and they come prepared with the right data and conclusions. Probing should be done before finalizing the decision to determine whether any key information still has not been brought to the table.

The third decision-making hurdle Charan identifies is "Piece-meal Perspectives." This occurs when participants refuse to look at the problem from the viewpoint of what is best for the company and see it only from the perspective of their particular function. This hurdle is overcome by repeatedly refocusing the group on the larger issue and admonishing the team members to take the broader view for the good of the overall organization.

Charan's final obstacle is the "Free-for-All." In this scenario the leader does not control the flow or direction of the meeting. Participants go off on tangents while others say nothing or obstinately stick to their opening positions. Fixing this issue is tough but necessary; the leader must tell the team how they can contribute positively to the discussion. He or she should reward those who do so and warn those who do not that negative behaviors will not be allowed.

Overcoming these decision-making impediments is key to making smart and timely decisions. Good leaders will recognize when these barriers are rising and move quickly to overcome them. From there they can move from decision to action, allocating resources and delegating tasks to implement team agreements.

### Fixing Major Problem Areas in Business

Washington's army suffered from many problems; lack of training, a broken supply system, and rapid turnover are just a few. Almost every business has problem areas that need to be fixed to make it more profitable. In IBM in the early 1990s more than a few fixes were needed; wholesale restructuring of the company was required. IBM was hemorrhaging billions of dollars and laying off thousands of employees. In January 1993, unable to right the corporate ship, IBM's CEO John Akers retired. Lou Gerstner was the man IBM's board brought in to bring the company back from the brink.

Gerstner was not an obvious choice. As he notes in his book *Who Says Elephants Can't Dance,* he didn't have a technology background and didn't feel that he was qualified. He also wasn't sure that IBM could survive its problems. Yet Gerstner was seen as a change agent by the hiring committee—one who could shake things up. Also, he had been a big IBM customer, which gave him the ability to see IBM's problems from the customer's viewpoint.

Once he accepted the job, Gerstner moved quickly to learn as much as possible. He visited several customers as well as major IBM locations, getting insights on what was wrong and what was working. Then he got down to business.

His first action was to reverse the previous regime's strategy of breaking up IBM. He believed there was a segment of the marketplace made of up of customers who wanted to look to one information technology (IT) vendor to meet their needs. In an industry with many specialized players, IBM could hold a differentiated position by being a complete hardware, software, and services vendor. IBM would be the one that could integrate solutions for customers that wanted to focus on things other than IT. Gerstner's thinking was counter to the prevailing opinions of pundits, but it was crucial to where he wanted to take IBM.

To keep IBM together it was critical to change the fundamentals of its business model. With red ink overflowing, maintaining the status quo was not an option. Revenue was dropping like a rock and margins were in freefall. To stabilize IBM Gerstner brought in Jerry York as chief financial officer. After doing the math, York put together a plan to cut almost $9 billion in expenses. It was painful and led to another 35,000 layoffs, but it allowed IBM to continue functioning as a viable entity. On top of the cuts Gerstner and York worked to reengineer the way IBM did business in its key processes. By consolidating IT systems, revamping the development process, and outsourcing non-core functions, they moved more billions out of the expense category to the bottom line.

Last, Gerstner sold off many assets that were not an essential part of IBM. This included expensive and underutilized real estate, most of the corporate planes, and IBM's large art collection that was mostly collecting dust in storage. He also looked at the different business units and sold those that were not central to his new strategy.

Through these actions Gerstner fixed the major operational problems facing IBM and saved it from bankruptcy. These steps then positioned IBM for its resurgence as an industry leader and a top-notch blue chip stock.

*Summary*

For Washington to execute his strategy he needed to **fix major organizational problems**. These included basics such as supply, logistics, and troop training. To help him, Washington **put together a winning team**. Despite interference by Congress, he for the most part selected the right officers; these were the men who would eventually lead the colonial army to victory. How the final victory would be achieved is the subject of our next chapter.

# 7 ▪ Securing Liberty

## *Victory through a Strong Alliance*

### *Thinking and Acting under Pressure*

Washington and the other colonial leaders knew that if America stood alone, Britain could focus all its war efforts on the young country to defeat the rebellion. An undistracted Britain, the foremost power in the world with the globe's strongest navy, could then marshal all its resources to bring the colonies to heel. Although France had only a few short years ago been the colonies' greatest enemy (and there was still significant distrust of her by many of America's leaders), she was the one card the fledgling country could play. Bringing France into the war would counterbalance Britain's navy, especially since ships-of-the-line belonging to France's ally Spain would also be added to the mix. Furthermore, the entry of France would mean the war would be global in nature. Britain's ministers and generals would now be forced to fight not only in America but in many other places also. The homeland would have to be defended as well as other colonial possessions such as the rich West Indies. Thus, American efforts to bring Britain's ancient enemy, France, into the war had been ongoing since the beginning of the Revolution.

France had other reasons for supporting the colonies against Britain beyond simple revenge for losing Canada and hatred based on hundreds of years of fighting. The loss of the American colonies and their trade would be a major blow to Britain's economy, which in turn would reduce her military might. This would allow a resurgence of French power and prestige in Europe, France's main area of interest. Last, France might be able to pick up one or two jewels in the form of colonial possessions or North Atlantic fishing grounds should Britain come out on the losing side of the war. These at least were the advantages the wily French foreign minister, Charles Gravier, Comte de Vergennes, presented to the young French king, Louis XVI.

The first official contact between France and the American colonies came in 1775 in, of all places, London. The linkage was between a French spy in Vergennes's employ, Caron de Beaumarchais, and Arthur Lee, an agent in the service of Massachusetts. Beaumarchais was an interesting character with many talents beyond spy craft. A man of humble birth, Beaumarchais had risen in favor in the royal court, partly through being a playwright (he authored both *The Barber of Seville* and *The Marriage of Figaro*). Lee pressed Beaumarchais to use his office to request arms and money from France to support the Revolution. Convinced this support would redound to the advantage of France, Beaumarchais worked with Vergennes to persuade the king. At first Louis XVI was reluctant to come to America's aid, fearing Britain's response, but eventually the arguments of Beaumarchais and Vergennes won him over in the spring of 1776. Shortly thereafter France provided one million livres for arms and other supplies for the colonies, using a fake business as a front to avoid a direct challenge to Britain. France's ally Spain also agreed to provide assistance to the Americans. To mask this covert assistance, France constantly reassured Britain of her enduring friendship.

With this initial assistance in hand Congress sent an official delegation to Paris headed by Benjamin Franklin. Arriving in December 1776 Franklin went about pursuing the colonies' interests by validating French assumptions about Americans. The French believed Americans to be simple and innocent, and Franklin played the role to the hilt. With simple dress and plain speech Franklin became wildly popular, gaining access to the finest salons in Paris to plead his case. His goal was recognition by France of the United States as well as a formal alliance with her. Despite Franklin's popularity, the French leadership was reluctant to openly support the colonies until they proved the Revolution had staying power. The king and his counselors were also concerned that the Americans might still find a way to reconcile with the mother country. So despite Franklin's efforts to nurture the relationship, nothing concrete happened for several months.

Although the news that Philadelphia had fallen reached France in late 1777, at roughly the same time word came of the American victory at Saratoga and the capture of an entire British Army. With that news France was convinced that the colonies could win, and in February 1778 France and the United States signed a treaty in which France officially recognized the new nation. France also agreed to give most-favored-nation status to the Americans. In the event of war between France and England (which was now inevitable), both France and the new country agreed to fight until American independence had been achieved, and neither would make a separate peace with London. Last, and very important to the Americans, France agreed not to reclaim any captured land in North America. This laid to rest colonial fears that France would seek to reestablish its empire at the expense of the young nation.

The British government, seeing that England stood alone and facing the likelihood of fighting on multiple fronts, sent a peace offer to the colonies. It addressed all the colonies' concerns but did not go as far as offering independence. Had this offer been made much earlier, America's leaders would have eagerly accepted it. Now, however, it fell on deaf ears, and they responded, "Acknowledge our Independence, or withdraw your fleets and armies and we will treat with you for peace and commerce." This Britain refused to do, and so the war continued.

While diplomatic moves came to conclusion in Europe, the war moved on in America. In May 1778 the British made a change in command, with General Clinton replacing General Howe as commander of all British troops in the colonies. Howe had never been very enthusiastic about carrying on the war in the colonies, and his replacement Clinton was not either. Clinton believed that "neither honor nor credit could be expected from it, but on the contrary a considerable portion of blame, however unmerited, seemed to be almost inevitable." In addition, Clinton would prove to have poor relations with other key British Army and Navy commanders, which would prove to be an issue in coming battles. Again, Providence would favor Washington with its choice of his opponents.

With the change of command came new orders from the British government to Clinton to abandon Philadelphia and move back to New York to await the results of Britain's peace offer to the colonies. Washington's spies soon learned of this and Washington knew that if the British did not have enough ships to take the army by sea they would have to cross in front of his army. In that case Washington was determined to attack them in a large-scale battle. His army had regained its strength and now had numbers roughly equal to those of his British opponent. Thanks to von Steuben the army was now better trained and because of Henry Knox it was very strong in artillery. Washington felt that this was the time to deal the British a blow strong enough to convince them that any chance of winning the war in America was gone.

In mid-June the British evacuated Philadelphia, with the army marching north to New York with Clinton at its head. Washington set out in pursuit, creating an advance guard of 6,000 men to track the British while the rest of the army followed. Originally naming Lafayette as its leader, Washington relented to protests about seniority by General Charles Lee (who had returned to the army after a prisoner exchange) and gave Lee command. While Lee, with his higher rank, could rightly claim the honor of leading the advance guard, putting him in charge of it would prove to be a mistake Washington would severely regret.

Lee made contact with the British Army on June 28 near Monmouth County Courthouse. Despite orders by Washington to press the attack Lee was hesitant, giving no orders to his officers and failing to tell the men where to form their lines. The British took advantage of the lack of American leadership, and Washington arrived on the scene to see his men confused and in retreat. Cursing Lee and sending him to the rear, Washington took control of the situation himself. In a calm and cool manner he organized the men on the field and set up new battle lines to receive the British assault. Once order was restored and with his army's front holding, Washington rode back to urge his remaining troops to hurry to the field to reinforce their comrades.

Clinton, being told the Americans were in disarray, resolved to attack them to seize the advantage. He launched one assault after another, but Washington's lines held, delivering volley after volley into the advancing British and Hessian troops as von Steuben had trained them to do. Eventually Clinton called off the attacks and both armies retired for the evening, spent from fighting. Although Clinton would be able to use the respite to continue his march unmolested to New York, Monmouth was claimed as a victory by the Americans. They had stood toe-to-toe with European regulars and held their ground. Washington, leading from the front to save the day, restored his image in the eyes not only of his army but of the country as well. While it was not a knockout blow to the British, Monmouth served notice that the war's momentum was now on the side of the Americans.

### First Attempts at Working with Allies

On July 10, 1778, France officially declared war on Great Britain. The entry of France into the war significantly changed Washington's strategy. Instead of merely trying to keep his army in the field and strike the occasional blow against the British, he could now take the initiative. France would not only be sending naval support but eventually thousands of well-trained French troops who would take the field with Washington's regulars and the militia. This was much welcome help, but coordinating with the

French would not be easy. Besides the language and cultural differences there was the lingering suspicion among the Americans of their traditional enemy. Having plans agreed on and executed was also a major challenge given the distances involved and the need to communicate via messenger. Unfortunately, the first attempt at a cooperative military venture would end in disappointment and recriminations, and it would take Washington's best efforts to keep the alliance intact.

The first military support provided by France took the form of a naval fleet led by the Comte d'Estaing. Washington had hoped d'Estaing would attack the Royal Navy fleet at New York, but the French admiral questioned whether he could get his ships across the bar at Sandy Hook and so declined that opportunity. The next chance for combined Franco-American operations was for d'Estaing to support an attack by Major General John Sullivan on Newport, Rhode Island. The British force there numbered 7,000 men who were under the command of Major General Sir Robert Pigot. The defeat of this force would not only deal a major physical blow to the British but a successful operation between the two new allies would provide a psychological advantage as well.

It was not to be. Although the French fleet was shadowed by Admiral Howe up the coast, the French admiral had the upper hand as he found shelter in a bay and did not have to come out to take on the British. Yet he chose to do so and went to sea, only to have his ships scattered by a storm. He gathered his ships together but he felt they were so battered that he could not stay to support Sullivan's attack. Instead he sailed to Boston to lick his wounds, hanging Sullivan out to dry and forcing him to retreat. A major opportunity had been lost.

Sullivan and his officers were obviously very frustrated and wrote a letter that questioned d'Estaing's honor. The French officers were also upset, feeling that the Americans knew nothing of war and yet were in the position to give orders to their French allies. Washington had to ask Lafayette to go back to France to calm things down. He also wrote to Sullivan, saying in part, "Prudence dictates that we should put the best face upon the matter and, to the World, attribute the movement to Boston, to necessity. The Reasons are too obvious to need explaining."

No other major operations were initiated in 1778 by the Americans, but the British had their own plans. At the urging of Lord George Germain, Clinton sought to widen the war by attacking the southern colonies. He hoped to find many Loyalists in the South who would rally to the king's banner, believing all that was needed was for the king's troops to win some victories and take cities as bases—and the South would revert to the Crown.

The first British move in the southern campaign was an attack on Savannah, Georgia. A small force led by Lieutenant Colonel Archibald Campbell landed at Savannah in late December 1778 and met an American contingent under Robert Howe on December 29. The much smaller American force met with disaster, losing a short battle and the city of Savannah with it. Another joint Franco-American effort to take it back in October 1779 failed, and d'Estaing was forced to leave America for France to avoid the coming hurricane season. Again, the new alliance had failed to yield results.

The next target for the British in the South was Charleston, South Carolina. It was the largest and most prosperous city in the region, and its fall would be a major loss for the Cause. Beyond the loss of the city, the surrender of so large a garrison was something Washington and the American Army could not afford. Unfortunately for the Americans, that's precisely what happened after a short siege.

Now that Clinton had achieved his aim of establishing a base in the Carolinas he turned over the job of subduing the rest of the South to Cornwallis and sailed back to New York. Meanwhile, in response to the loss of Charleston, Congress nominated General Gates to take command of the southern American Army and oppose Cornwallis, disregarding Washington's recommendation of Nathanael Greene for the position. It would be a choice they would soon regret.

Horatio Gates, the hero of Saratoga, took the leadership of a small, dispirited force in North Carolina. Like its cousin in the

North, the southern army suffered from lack of supplies and food. Gates, eager for action, did little to prepare the army for battle, instead immediately putting it on the road with Charleston as its objective. At a place called Camden, Gates found the British, and after a sharp battle with the British regulars, his militia-heavy force crumbled. As the situation worsened Gates did not step forward to halt the flood to the rear but instead fled from the field himself. Racing away on his horse he did not halt until he had traveled almost 200 miles from the scene of his defeat.

The situation in the South was now dire for the Americans. The defeated army had for the most part dissolved, and Gates was relieved of command. It would fall to bands of irregular American forces combined with a revitalized army led by Nathanael Greene to restore the fortunes of the Cause in the South (Congress, having seen that their estimation of Gates was woefully incorrect, now accepted Washington's nomination of Greene to lead what was left of the army in the Carolinas).

Despite British victories the population as a whole did not rally to the support the Crown. Instead Cornwallis found his forces besieged by guerrilla leaders such as Francis Marion, the "Swamp Fox." These small partisan units attacked British supply trains and outposts, limiting British control of the countryside and keeping Cornwallis in the dark on the movements of his opponents. The British responded by unleashing Benastre Tarleton, who would hunt down the guerrillas and destroy communities that supported them. It was Tarleton and his men who were responsible for what became known as "Waxhaw's Massacre," in which American troops who were beaten and tried to surrender were instead cut down. This approach by the British served to make the war in the South more bloody and savage than it had been in the North and increased resistance to the king's cause instead of helping it.

Indeed, the war in the South was turning against the British, and they suffered two severe defeats in October 1779 and January 1780. Cornwallis, seeking to extend British control in the Carolinas, sent a strong Tory force under British Major Patrick Ferguson with orders to pacify the area. Ferguson's detachment was surrounded and destroyed at King's Mountain by the rebels.

Cornwallis then sent out Benastre Tarleton to try and run to ground an American army under Daniel Morgan. Tarleton's force attacked Morgan's mix of Continentals and militia at a place called Cowpens, but Morgan, using smart tactics, bloodily repulsed Tarleton's men and emerged victorious.

Hearing of Tarleton's defeat, Cornwallis attempted to recover by tracking down Morgan, but the British general moved too slowly. Cornwallis, hoping to match the American Army's mobility, now made a major decision that would have great consequences for the war. He burned his baggage and even consigned his army's tents and rum to the fire, all with the intent of enabling his men to catch the American Army. This done, he set off after the main army, now commanded by Nathanael Greene.

What followed was a campaign in which Cornwallis sought to bring Greene to battle while Greene strove to avoid one. Greene, aware that he must keep his army intact if there was a hope of winning back the South, would always keep one step ahead of Cornwallis. Only after Greene was reinforced with extra men from Virginia and North Carolina did he decide to end his will-o'-the-wisp strategy and give battle to Cornwallis at Guilford Court House in North Carolina. In a confusing and intense battle fought primarily in the woods, the two sides struggled for the advantage. At one point, when it appeared to Cornwallis that the American line would overcome his, he ordered his artillery to fire into the massed men. This served to force the two lines apart, after which the British re-formed and drove Greene's army from the field. Although the British held the field they had suffered terrible losses, and Greene's army, though battered, remained a force to be reckoned with.

Cornwallis, now looking at his next step, focused on Virginia. He had thought for a long while that the war could be won if Virginia could be taken, and he had written to Clinton asserting such a strategy. Now following his own strategy, Cornwallis decided to move north to Virginia to link up with British forces there under the traitorous Benedict Arnold, hoping that Clinton himself might join him. Meanwhile, Greene moved south and in a series of battles was able to reclaim almost all of the Carolinas and

Georgia for the Cause. All the Crown had left were garrisons in Charleston and Savannah, but the countryside was lost.

## Washington Makes the Alliance Work for Victory

Washington's choice of Greene for command in the South had been a wise one for the course of the war. Washington himself had not been idle either. He had welcomed the arrival of a French Army under the Comte de Rochambeau in Newport, Rhode Island, in July 1780. Rochambeau was nominally under Washington's command, so the command situation was clear and workable, but there were still problems. Language was one barrier; Rochambeau did not speak English and Washington did not speak French. Washington sought to overcome this problem by appointing the trusted Lafayette to be his liaison to the French commander. However, instead of improving the situation it made things worse. Although Lafayette held a high command in the American Army he had only been a captain in France, and he was very young and inexperienced compared to Rochambeau and the French general's officers. Eventually the difficulties were made clear to Washington and the situation was resolved by having the two commanders hold discussions directly.

Another problem was the difference between the two armies. The American Army had suffered greatly during the previous winter in Morristown, New Jersey, more than ever before. It was now in an extremely weakened state, the men poorly clothed and fed and looking most unmilitary. In contrast, the professional French troops looked like a real army in their elegant uniforms, and their officers were dressed brilliantly. Furthermore, lack of pay had led to mutinies by American troops against Congress, and these were put down with a mixture of actions taken to address the men's concerns and harsh discipline in which some ringleaders were executed (while Washington was always concerned with the care of his men, he never tolerated insubordination). In such a situation it was difficult for the French to take the Americans seriously.

Despite these problems the alliance moved forward. Washington himself greatly impressed the French, primarily with personal traits such as his horsemanship, great physical stature, and presence. One French officer described his first meeting with Washington thus: "His dignified address, his simplicity of manners, and mild gravity surpassed our expectation and won every heart." Over time they would also gain more respect for him as they saw how he handled the many challenges he faced with resolution and by his always proper and friendly interactions with them.

Washington had hoped to work with Rochambeau to mount an attack on Clinton in New York, but after much consideration, that strategy was considered to have meager prospects of success. However, now that Greene was in a position to secure the majority of that region and Cornwallis had moved north to Virginia, the dynamics of the war changed. They changed further when Washington and Rochambeau learned that a French fleet under Comte de Grasse was headed for the West Indies and might be available for operation in the Americas. The two commanders agreed to forgo an attack on New York and instead link their forces with de Grasse to attack Cornwallis's men now operating near Chesapeake Bay in Virginia. The hope was to capture Cornwallis and his men by cornering him on land and preventing his escape by sea.

The plan was in place, but serious obstacles remained. The logistics of coordinating with the French fleet so that it arrived on the spot at roughly the same time as the two armies was problematic to say the least. Even should the word get to de Grasse in time, the weather would have to cooperate for him to make it safely to the Chesapeake. He would also have to either avoid or defeat any Royal Navy ships in the process. Another problem was Clinton; he would have to be convinced an attack on New York was imminent in order to avoid his reinforcing Cornwallis or attacking the allied army on its march south. Also, the Franco-American army would have to march almost 800 miles from its current position in the north down to Virginia. Last, Cornwallis himself might choose to take action on his own and move to another position. Yet with all these factors in mind, Washington and Rochambeau believed this was the best opportunity to end the war, and thus together they rolled the dice.

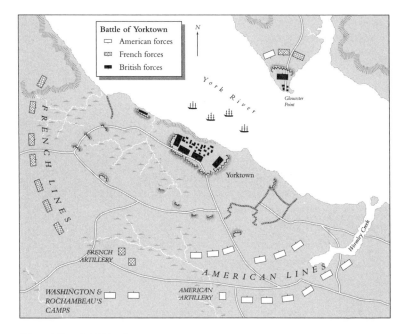

Adapted from britishbattles.com.

In early August Washington learned from Lafayette (who had been sent to Virginia with troops to keep an eye on Cornwallis) that the British general had moved his army to Yorktown on the Chesapeake. This was good news as it set up the opportunity to trap Cornwallis according to the plan. Washington and Rochambeau then set off to Virginia after making demonstrations and spreading rumors that led Clinton to believe New York was still Washington's aim. The two also maintained security by keeping the allied army's objective a secret shared with only the top echelon of officers; the men were not told of their ultimate destination until the operation was well under way.

Washington and Rochambeau arrived at Yorktown in mid-September to link up with Lafayette. Once there they were relieved to see de Grasse's fleet anchored off Yorktown; all they had known previously was that de Grasse had arrived in Chesapeake but then had left to fight a British fleet. On the enemy side, the majority of Cornwallis's men had built fortifications to defend Yorktown itself while the rest of his command was across the York River in Gloucester. Unless Cornwallis could get relief from the sea (now doubtful as the British fleet in the area had been driven off), Washington had his opponent cornered.

Why had Cornwallis, an experienced British general, allowed himself to be trapped in such a fashion? Communications between Cornwallis and Clinton contained much bickering over strategy, and numerous letters between the two had led to confusion and acrimony. In the end a frustrated Clinton finally ordered Cornwallis to select a position in Virginia and hold it. When Lafayette's small force arrived on the scene Cornwallis likely felt little threatened, and based on all his prior experience in the war, he knew he could rely on the Royal Navy either to bring him reinforcements from Clinton or to allow him to escape by sea. Unfortunately for him, the entry of France and the French fleet into the war had made that experience and thinking both irrelevant and ultimately fatal.

On September 28, 1781, the allied army began to take up positions around Yorktown and Gloucester, setting up siege lines that would surround the British. The British Army had roughly 7,500 men and faced a combined allied army of 16,000 soldiers and 800 French marines. While Cornwallis had built both outer and inner fortifications at Yorktown, he ended up abandoning his outer works on September 29, fearing he did not have the strength to defend them. This allowed the French and American troops to move close to Yorktown and set up their artillery for a bombardment of the British there.

Although the British began firing their cannon first, the allied army worked quickly to deploy its artillery and by October 9 was ready to respond. Washington himself fired the first shot, and soon numerous French and American cannonballs were falling on British positions in rapid succession. Thanks to Henry Knox and his French counterpart, the allied army had a preponderance of artillery, and it soon began to tell, rapidly putting the British guns out of commission and destroying the British works.

On October 14 a combined assault on two British redoubts featured fierce hand-to-hand fighting before the two small forts fell to the allies. A British sortie on October 16 failed to push the allied lines back, and the British position now became desperate. Cornwallis, who had hoped for help from Clinton, now realized his only chance was to evacuate Yorktown by rowing his men across the York River to Gloucester and hope to break out there. On the night of the October 16 the British attempted the crossing, but to their dismay, a heavy storm broke and made the evacuation impossible. Cornwallis had run out of options and the following day he sent a flag of truce to Washington.

After agreeing to terms, the British Army marched out of Yorktown to surrender on October 19, 1781, passing through the French and American troops, each lining one side of the road. According to some accounts they stepped to the tune of a song called "The World Turned Upside Down." If the anecdote is true, it was a fitting tribute to the circumstances in which they found themselves.

With Cornwallis claiming to be ill (and thus avoiding the ignominy of surrender), the British were led by General Charles O'Hara. He tried to surrender his sword to the Frenchman Rochambeau but was told that Washington was the commander-in-chief. Washington then signaled to O'Hara that he should present it to General Benjamin Lincoln, the American commander who had been defeated at Charleston and who was Washington's second in command. That evening, after the British had laid down their arms, Washington hosted a dinner for the top-ranking officers from the three nations.

The loss of another army in the Americas would prove to be too much for the British government and populace. Eventually, seeking to end the war (which had now become a global conflict), Britain would agree to terms in 1782 that would not only give America independence but grant rights that would eventually lead to the nation's westward expansion. Washington, who had such a large role in the battle for independence, would also play a role in the country's growth. However, for the time being on October 19, 1781, Washington could feel proud of what he and his ragtag army had achieved.

## Thinking and Acting under Pressure in Business

At the Battle of Monmouth, Washington had to think and act under great pressure. With the battle in jeopardy because of an irresponsible General Lee, Washington took personal control of the troops, reorganized their battle line, and repulsed the repeated British assaults. With the training Washington ensured they were given by von Steuben, the Americans held the field and won the respect of the British regulars.

In business, it is obviously crucial to be able to deal with pressure, make quick decisions, rally the troops, and win. And no situation requires those abilities more than a business turnaround. Most times the company is reeling from declining revenue, increased losses, and a poor market and industry image. Outside observers are taking potshots at the company. Internally the employees are spending time wondering what will happen to their jobs, and executives and management are likely sending out their resumes. The company needs to be turned around quickly, but a new strategy to win must be developed, pragmatic action plans put in place, employees energized, and customers and shareholders reassured. All this must be done most times by someone brought in from the outside who has a very short time after taking the job to understand the business realities.

This was the situation Carlos Ghosn faced when he was named Nissan's new CEO in 1999. Ghosn, a Renault executive, got the job after Renault purchased controlling interest in the Japanese auto manufacturer and named him to head the company. To complicate Ghosn's turnaround job, he was not only taking over a new company but doing so in a different country and culture. Japanese society resisted job cuts in favor of long-term employment, and the country was a difficult place for foreign executives to succeed. Other companies had considered buying Nissan but had recoiled at the costs involved and the low probability of making the company profitable.

What Ghosn found at Nissan was a company weighed down by $17 billion in debt, falling in market share, and hemorrhaging losses measured in billions year after year. The culture was one that allowed management promotions regardless of disastrous results; the employees were confused about the company's strategy to win in the marketplace and cynical about its ability to regain its footing.

Despite the difficulties, Ghosn, like Washington, brought assets with him. He had experience dealing with and adapting to new situations and different cultures—he was born in Brazil and had attended school in Lebanon and France. His early life had taught him to deal with change and its stresses, and he had an interest in and curiosity about people who were different from him. Ghosn also had been in turnaround situations, having successfully executed them when he was an executive at Michelin and within Renault itself. Last, he felt that he could turn the weakness of coming from outside Japanese culture into a strength, as he could execute hard actions such as layoffs and have them accepted more easily as a foreigner than could a Japanese leader.

To succeed he had to move fast. He knew one key to success was to clear up the confusion on the strategy by delivering a solid plan to revive the company's fortunes. Explaining the turnaround Ghosn said, "One of the biggest signs that a company is in trouble is when the employees are confused about strategy and priorities. My first act was to move from a state of confusion to one of clarification. I needed to explain what we had to undertake and why we had to undertake it and then outline the best way to do it." So in three short months Ghosn developed and communicated the "Nissan Revival Plan" to get the business back on its feet. He did not bring in a predetermined plan but instead spent a good deal of time listening to voices both inside and outside Nissan. While he did not agree with all the suggestions (many suggested too tentative an approach), he wanted to make sure he had heard all possibilities.

Ghosn's plan included cutting 21,000 employees, closing plants, significantly dropping the number of suppliers, and reducing parts costs. These actions were painful, but they were necessary to stop the losses and give the rest of Nissan a chance at survival. But while these steps slowed the bleeding, by themselves they were insufficient to revive the patient. To increase revenues Ghosn realized he had to deliver much better products to the marketplace than Nissan had done previously. In 1999 Nissan's car and truck lines were lackluster at best; they lacked inspiration and excitement and had no features or design that differentiated them from the myriad of other vehicles in the market. So the new CEO put great emphasis on bringing out great products that would have strong appeal to buyers in different product segments. Ghosn's philosophy is this: "We don't want to be something for everybody, we want to be everything for some people. By that definition, we're going to distinguish ourselves." Recognizing that great design is crucial to delivering great products, Ghosn raised the importance and standing of this specialty, saying, "Our designers are talented, and they also are working in an environment where the role of design is recognized." The new emphasis on design resulted in popular new releases such as the Nissan Z, Altima, Armada, Murano, Titan, and the separate Infiniti luxury brand.

To make his plan work, Ghosn, like Washington, had to be both demanding of his troops and encouraging as well. To inspire his employees Ghosn made sure that he connected with them, speaking with and listening to them one-on-one directly and, since Nissan was a large company, through companywide communications. Although he didn't speak Japanese, Ghosn, like Washington with the French, still found meaningful ways to connect and inspire. For example, he told employees that he and his new executive team would fire themselves if they didn't achieve the Revival Plan goals. Again, like General Washington, Ghosn put himself in the line of fire, winning the confidence of employees that he was serious about turning things around.

Although he was a facts and numbers person, Ghosn also displayed passion about cars. He had loved autos since his childhood and could recognize different models at a very young age by something as arcane as the unique sounds of their horns. Ghosn radiated this love of the industry to all his employees, yet he did not let his passion for cars lead him to make emotion-driven decisions about them. "Now am I a car lover? Yes. Am I a car fanatic? No. Which means I will never make a wrong business decision just because I love a car." By 2005, Nissan had increased market share, attained the best profitability in the industry (as measured by operating margins), and posted a stock price that rose about $5 in 1999 to the mid-$20s. And these numbers led to Ghosn's winning the top job at Renault in 2005 to become the CEO of both Nissan and Renault. Doing for Renault what he did for Nissan will be a big challenge for Ghosn, and the jury is still out at the time of this writing. But if he exhibits the same leadership capabilities at Renault as he did at Nissan, his chances of success are excellent.

## Managing Alliances in Business

Achieving an alliance with the French was crucial in helping the colonies win the war and secure their independence from the British. Once the alliance was achieved, it fell to Washington to turn it into victory on the battlefield. He had to overcome language difficulties, cultural differences, diverse war aims, and time and distance challenges to win the battle at Yorktown and eventually the war. To maintain the alliance with France and make it effective, Washington had to nurture and foster its growth as well as overcome problems when they occurred. When the alliance's first joint action between the Comte d'Estaing and General Sullivan failed and ended in recriminations and finger-pointing, Washington did what was necessary to calm down both sides and move forward. He ensured that his men and the French knew how important and beneficial the relationship was to each country. When Washington had the opportunity to work directly with the French in his relationship with the Comte de Rochambeau, he reached out to them in the best way he knew how: sending Lafayette as the intermediary. When he realized that approach was the wrong one, he didn't take offense. Instead he quickly changed tactics and rectified the situation by working one-on-one with Rochambeau. And it was Washington's personal presence and stature that was important to ensuring that the French took the Americans seriously and remained allies.

Business alliances often have many of the same issues; two companies come together with the objective of winning in the marketplace, but each brings to the table its own unique culture, history, goals, objectives, and views about how the alliance will work and what it is intended to achieve. Thus it is no surprise that so many mergers ultimately fail to gain their expected results and return the investment made.

One company that has been very successful at making alliances to create a marketplace winner has been Apple, with its iPod and iTunes business model. The iPod, with its elegant design and simplicity, has been a great hit with consumers. As of this writing, if you want to be hip, the only portable media player to carry is the iPod. But without iTunes, which lets iPod users download favorite songs on their personal computer easily for only ninety-nine cents, the iPod would not have been such a success. Although the iPod was introduced in 2001, its sales did not take off until iTunes became widely available in 2003.

To make iTunes work, Apple, led by its CEO and computer industry icon Steve Jobs, had to develop a mutually beneficial relationship with music companies and artists to create the new business model reflected in Apple's music store. The music industry feared downloading because companies like Napster had allowed pirated copies to be shared by millions of people without the music companies or artists seeing a penny of revenue for their work. And consumers who were used to pirating songs had to have an option to get songs that, while not free, could be purchased at a reasonable cost.

So Jobs linked up with major record labels to sell a host of their songs through iTunes. To do so, Jobs not only had to give them the majority of the revenue from the sale (about 65 percent) but he also had to break an Apple taboo by making iTunes work for Microsoft Windows PC users. In allowing the music companies the lion's share of the song revenue Jobs sold more of the highly profitable iPods. With this strategy Jobs and the music industry gained access to the vast majority of personal computer owners.

For former music pirates, the ability to easily and simply get their most wanted tunes legally for less than a dollar and have this work on the coolest MP3 player was a no-brainer. So with the compelling combination of the great-looking iPod and the simple and inexpensive iTunes music store, Apple's sales soared. By the end of 2003 Apple said it had sold 25 million songs since the introduction of iTunes in April of that year. By the end of 2006 more than 1.5 billion songs had been sold through iTunes and Apple's online music store accounted for over 80 percent of sales of downloaded music. Meanwhile, the iPod continues to be far and away the leading portable media player, by itself claiming about 70 percent of sales in the category as of 2006.

The combined success of iPod and the iTunes' alliances has led to further alliances—Apple has worked with several car manufacturers to make their cars iPod capable, with 70 percent of the 2007 car models iPod ready. And now shoes, backpacks, and clothing are being manufactured to make them "iPod ready." All this has paid off in the stock price, with Apple's share price rising from about $8 in 2003 to around $80 by 2006, a tenfold increase. Job's ability to show those in the music industry how to overcome their fears and see a future in which their and Apple's joint interests could pay off was critical to this historic business victory.

## Summary

At Monmouth, Washington showed that he could **think and act under pressure**, turning a near defeat into a solid performance. Washington personally took control of the battle and regained the initiative for the Continental Army. His dynamic leadership in a high-stakes and time-constrained environment was key to success.

The failures of Lee at Monmouth and Gates at Camden (both of whom Washington saw as poor leaders who were forced upon him) showed again that Washington had a good sense of which of his subordinates could perform and which could not.

In working with the French, Washington displayed different traits, acting diplomatically to **manage the alliance** between the two countries to keep it intact and ensure that it would eventually be victorious.

These traits and others would prove crucial as Washington moved to the next stage of his career and his pivotal role in America's journey to freedom and self-government. The next step in the journey is told in the following chapter.

# 8 ▪ Statesman

*Leading through Wisdom
and Integrity*

## Saving the Cause: Integrity

With the victory at Yorktown in late 1781 it appeared to all that
Britain's will to continue the war would eventually wane, resulting in American independence. However, Washington was
concerned that this very view would allow Congress, the states,
and the populace to stop supporting the army just as victory was
in its grasp. Indeed, Congress continued to provide such limited
funding to the troops that the army could barely maintain itself in
the field as the move toward a negotiated peace progressed.

Washington now had to deal not only with the army's logistical problems but its morale as well. Previously it was the men who
were disgruntled, but now the officers were also becoming upset.
Lack of action and interminable waiting were difficult, but the
larger issues for the officers were concern for their futures and
dissatisfaction with recognition of their past sacrifices. Congress

was not forthcoming with back pay owed to many of the officers and seemed to be wavering on a prior pledge of pensions for them. While other men had gone about their daily lives, the Continental officers had put their lives and fortunes on the line, at great personal and financial sacrifice. Washington, upset at this treatment of the men he had served with for so long under such difficult conditions, was concerned about its repercussions: "I cannot avoid apprehending that a train of evils will follow of a very serious and distressing nature."

His fears were valid and prophetic. As discontent rose among the officer corps and talk rumbled about threatening Congress with military action, Washington persuaded the men to petition the legislature instead. Unfortunately, this approach did not work. The states had denied Congress the power to directly tax the people, and thus the legislative body could not raise the funds to meet the officers' demands.

A core group of officers began discussing the need for direct action. Frustrated by their poor treatment and motivated to increase the power of the central government at the expense of the states, these officers planned to install a military tyranny or even a kingship with Washington at its head. Knowing that Washington was the one man in the country who was crucial to their plan, the group asked Alexander Hamilton in February 1783 to write to Washington to convince him to join their plot. Hamilton focused his argument on the need for temporary actions by the army that would convince the states of the necessity for a strong central government. At the same time, Washington received a letter from a congressman warning him that several officers were plotting to destroy his reputation should he oppose their plans.

Washington was frustrated to see his officers and men so poorly treated, especially as he had convinced them to remain steadfast and give him time to work with Congress to achieve justice. Furthermore, he too saw the need for a strong central government. Yet he also knew that a move toward a military tyranny would destroy the very cause he had been fighting for. So in early March he responded to Hamilton's letter, telling him in no uncertain terms that he would not support the officers' plan.

The officers now determined to move forward without Washington and began circulating letters widely to enlist others in what would become known as the "Newburgh Conspiracy" based on the location of the army's camp in Newburgh, New York. Furthermore, they called for a meeting of all the officers without Washington's consent to engage them in their efforts. In response, Washington sent his own letter disapproving of the officers' assembly and announced his own meeting for March 15, 1783.

When Washington appeared at the scene he saw that many of the men who had previously seen him as their leader now considered him an obstacle to be removed. Washington spoke to the officers, calling the unapproved meeting "unmilitary" and "subversive of all order and discipline." He then addressed the arguments being circulated, urging the men not to follow their "insidious purposes" and instead trust in the legislative body to address their concerns. The speech ended with an appeal to their patriotism and virtue in the hope of quelling their anger.

The men were not convinced. Seeing this, Washington pulled from his pocket a letter from Congressman Joseph Jones. After a fumbling attempt to read it, Washington took out a pair of reading glasses, stating, "Gentlemen, you will permit me to put on my spectacles, for I have not only grown gray but almost blind in the service of my country."

This act and its accompanying words from the heart did what his prepared speech had not done. Washington's emotional appeal reminded his officers of his own sacrifices and won them back to his side and that of the republic. Eventually a more conciliatory approach would be taken by the officers, and Congress, seeing the need to be responsive to the army, would meet most of the officers' demands.

When the official peace treaty ending the war was finally signed in Paris in September 1783, Washington took the next steps toward turning power back to Congress. After leading the army into New York City as the British evacuated it in late 1783, Washington disbanded the troops and said a tearful farewell to those officers who had served with him so faithfully during the long struggle. He then rode to Annapolis, Maryland, where

Congress was sitting. All along the way he was hailed as the conquering hero. Finally reaching Annapolis, Washington submitted his resignation as the commander-in-chief of the army on December 23, 1783, in another emotional ceremony: "Having now finished the work assigned me, I retire from the great theatre of Action; and bidding an Affectionate farewell to this August body under whose orders I have so long acted, I here offer my Commission, and take my leave of all the employments of public life." Washington then set out for Mount Vernon, reaching it on New Year's Eve, with the intent of enjoying a well-earned retirement from public life.

Supported by his popularity among the people and the loyalty of the army, Washington could easily have let his ambitions overrule his integrity and become America's new king. Instead he chose the path that would set the future of the country, not only saving the fledgling republic but providing the example for America's future military leaders on the primacy of the civilian government and the importance of putting the needs of the country first. Events would soon cut short his private life and bring him back into the public service he had hoped to leave.

### Facilitating the Birth of the Constitution:
### Leading in a New Way

Washington had hoped to spend his time improving his Mount Vernon plantation and experimenting in agricultural pursuits. He also wanted to supervise the large tracts of land he had purchased in the west as well as explore a venture to build a canal on the Potomac to increase trade.

However, the newly formed United States was not living up to its name. Each state was following its own path and had not given Congress the funds or revenue sources needed to retire the massive debt created by the war. And under the Articles of Confederation, Congress had no power to tax citizens directly. Furthermore, the central government was proving too weak to project American power into the newly acquired territories in the west. The British had kept their outposts on the Great Lakes and in the

Ohio River Valley. Meanwhile, Spain closed the lower Mississippi to American trade. These factors made it difficult for the economy to expand and also raised concerns that settlers moving west would either set up their own independent states or align with the European countries. Sectional differences between North and South also held up progress on actions to improve the economy.

Washington recognized the weaknesses of the Articles of Confederation, stating in a letter, "The confederation appears to me to be little more than a shadow without the substance, and Congress a nugatory body, their ordinances being little attended to. . . . The wheels of government are clogged, and our brightest prospects and that high expectation which was entertained of us by the wondering world are turned into astonishment, and from the high ground on which we stood we are descending into the vale of confusion and darkness."

The differences between the states were hindering Washington in his desire to develop a canal on the Potomac. Because the canal would affect multiple states, he needed them to agree on various issues regarding the project. He thus convened what became known as the Mount Vernon Conference, at which Maryland and Virginia resolved a number of disagreements to facilitate the project and enhance trade. The success of the conference led Virginia to propose a conference of all the states in 1786 at Annapolis to work on their joint commercial interests. At that session, urged by a letter from Washington, the five attending states called for yet another conference of all the states to fix the inadequacies of the Articles of Confederation that had been ratified by the Continental Congress in 1781 as a first attempt to bind the states together. The new conference, to be held in Philadelphia, would become known as the Constitutional Convention.

Before the convention could take place an event occurred that would greatly influence its proceedings. Farmers in Massachusetts, hurt by the colony's economic policies that favored eastern businesses over western agriculture, led a short but violent uprising. Called "Shays's Rebellion" after one of its leaders, Daniel P. Shays, a veteran of the Revolutionary War, the armed movement was quickly put down. But it created an emotional impetus and imparted a sense of urgency to the upcoming convention, showing that significant steps to fix the government structure were needed to stave off anarchy.

By agreement, the delegates were to meet in Philadelphia in May 1787. Washington, who had strongly supported the convention, hoped to remain apart from the actual conference. Asked to lead Virginia's delegation, he found the request so agonizing he actually became ill. He wanted to remain in private life and did not want to be accused of trying to foster his own ambitions again since he'd so recently laid down the reins of power. Yet he also did not want to be seen as sitting idly on the sidelines and perhaps be held responsible for the convention's failure by refusing to be present. Finally, realizing he had little choice but to attend, Washington prepared by researching the history of ancient and current governments with the goal of developing basic principles he could promote. He set out for Philadelphia on May 9, arriving in the city on May 13. In two weeks enough delegates had arrived to constitute a quorum, and one of their first acts was to elect Washington president of the convention by unanimous vote.

His presence, based on his prior service to the country, added stature to the meeting. Although he brought no specific ideas for reorganizing the government, he did have the experience of his recent commercial activities and also his dealings with Congress and the states during the war. He felt strongly that the central government required more power than the Articles of Confederation allowed. Therefore he supported his Virginia delegation's proposal for a more powerful federal government composed of three branches of government. The convention agreed early to drop the Articles of Confederation in favor of the basics of the "Virginia Plan."

Washington's role in the convention was threefold. He brought legitimacy and prestige to the proceedings, which would prove critical to acceptance of the new Constitution. He elicited new ideas and promoted discussion from the delegates, ensuring that all felt they had had a part in drafting the new and important document. This role was crucial in reducing the friction that would inevitably arise among accomplished men from different states with different interests and philosophies. Rather than dominate the proceedings to promote his own ideas, Washington steered the group through disagreement to concurrence. His final role was to provide counsel on the formation of the new government based on his military, governmental, and business experience. The delegates sought his input especially on the role of the executive branch. This was a particular sticking point; it was clear that a stronger executive was needed but the old fear of tyranny remained. Washington's words as well as the example he had set during his wartime service and how he had handled the powers given him during the war played a major role here.

Once the convention agreed on the Constitution, Washington, like the other delegates, found it imperfect, yet said it was the "best Constitution that can be obtained at this Epoca." So he hoped for its approval by the states. If all did not ratify it, the entire proposal might fall apart. Given the spirited debate, Washington at times wanted to intercede on the Constitution's behalf as each state went through the ratification process. Yet he realized that it would be better for him to be in the background as the people debated. In the end the Constitution was ratified, much to Washington's relief. That such a document could not only be created and ratified but also serve so well over more than two centuries was due in large part to Washington's stature, practical experience, and facilitation. Had he not lent his prestige and efforts to the convention, it is certainly questionable if the gathering would have occurred, much less given birth to the document that became the foundation of the new republic. As James Monroe wrote to Thomas Jefferson, "Be assured [Washington's] influence carried this government."

### Integrity in Business

Washington always strove to act with integrity, concerned that everything he did would have neither appearance nor reality of impropriety. Rejecting a kingship and stopping the move toward tyranny were probably his most impressive and honorable acts. In the long term, his ethics and morals paid off not just for the country but for his career as well. Had he cut corners as commander-in-chief by mishandling the army's funds or by overreaching his authorized power, Congress would not have trusted him to continue in that position much less become the first president of the new nation (or for that matter, trust the executive branch with as much power as it did).

While most business leaders are ethical (or at the least not overly unethical), we have recent cases of accounting fraud scandals by Enron and WorldCom, and Tyco's securities fraud case. Other such examples are all too frequent through history when executives' motivation to maximize profits, get quick returns, and enrich themselves leads them astray.

Yet in 1982, James Burke, CEO of Johnson & Johnson (J&J), showed that the right motives and ethical actions can pay off financially. In September of that year seven people in the Chicago area died of cyanide poisoning. By putting together facts from the different cases, analysts discovered that the poison had been in capsules of the pain reliever Extra-Strength Tylenol. Immediately people in Chicago and around the nation were told to avoid the capsules. The result was a panic, made worse when other Tylenol capsules were found to be tampered with.

Due to Burke's foresight, J&J was prepared to handle such a crisis ethically. The heart of Johnson & Johnson's credo since its founding was its promise to customers. Developed by Robert Johnson in 1943 the credo affirmed in simple fashion, "We believe our first responsibility is to doctors, nurses and patients, to mothers and fathers and all others who use our products and services." In the mid-1970s Burke, believing the company had drifted away from this belief, challenged his team to either live up to the credo or quit saying it. In a series of meetings they debated its usefulness and in the end, recommitted to it. So when the Tylenol crisis came in the early 1980s, J&J as an organization was ready to live up its promise.

After learning that poison-laced Extra-Strength Tylenol capsules were causing the deaths, Johnson & Johnson quickly checked to see if the tampering was happening in their plants. The facts showed that the capsules leaving the plants were clean, indicating that someone had bought the capsules, added the poison, and then put the lethal bottles back on retail shelves (the final investigation would prove that this was indeed the case and involved the original tamperer and a number of copycats).

The poisoning was clearly not Johnson & Johnson's fault, so they might have tried to convince customers of this to protect their sales of Tylenol in the short term. Instead Burke and J&J management took a more ethical approach—one with integrity: They put customer safety first.

As a first step Johnson & Johnson worked with the media to get out as many facts as possible. Rather than retreat or stonewall by showing that its own plants were clear, J&J spread the word via the media telling customers not to take Tylenol already on the shelves until the company could ensure a safe product. They also instituted a nationwide recall of 31 million bottles of Tylenol, worth an estimated $100 million. Simultaneously, the company cooperated with the authorities (the FDA, the FBI, and the local police) to help solve the mystery. This, and putting public safety over profits, won them praise in the popular media.

Many industry observers thought this would be the end of Tylenol. Almost no one outside of J&J believed the previously strong and very profitable brand could overcome the cyanide-tampering scare. Yet Johnson & Johnson believed it could bounce back once the panic subsided if the company took the right actions.

To guarantee consumer safety J&J put Tylenol into tamper-proof bottles that were triple sealed. Then the company began a massive advertising, promotion, and PR campaign to reassure customers that Tylenol was safe again and still delivered great pain relief. Because of its prior positive dealings with the media, J&J was able to augment its efforts exponentially through free press to get the word out about Tylenol.

In the end, the ethical actions of Burke and Johnson & Johnson kept the Tylenol brand strong. At the time of the crisis, Tylenol had about 38 percent market share, which fell to about 8 percent immediately after the poison scare. But by acting with integrity J&J was soon able to recover its lost share and make Tylenol the market leader once again.

Recently, although it wasn't a safety issue, Toyota took steps to improve customer satisfaction with its new Corolla models by delaying their launch to ensure high quality. In 2006 Toyota had uncharacteristic quality problems caused by fast growth and some design issues. However, by acknowledging the problem and correcting it, Toyota has continued to be held in high regard and to maintain market share.

## Leading in New Ways

Probably the most popular image of George Washington in many people's minds is the fearless general standing in the boat in Emanuel Leutze's famous painting *Washington Crossing the Delaware*. In the painting Washington is resolutely looking to the far shore as he prepares for his assault on Trenton. He is the model of the charismatic, action-oriented leader, inspiring his men to overcome great obstacles to win victory. This is how leadership is often portrayed in business and indeed how many business leaders see themselves.

Washington could indeed play this role. He did it at Trenton and many other battlefields. When the situation demanded it, when the army was in danger, when time was at a premium and inspiration was a necessity, Washington personally rallied the troops, fearlessly braving bullets to lead his men to triumph. Yet that is not the only type of leadership Washington displayed.

Before the battle Washington would hold councils of war with his key officers, eliciting their opinions on the right course of action and listening to all points of view before deciding what action to take. This free discussion of all the officers' ideas helped Washington get them all on the same page with the strategy chosen.

In the Constitutional Convention, while Washington was chosen to lead it, he knew he could not simply issue orders to the men who were gathered in Philadelphia to draft the foundation of the nation's government. Another type of leadership was required, and Washington applied it. Treating the delegates from the various states as equals, Washington facilitated the conversation and helped shepherd it to a successful conclusion. He brought out the delegates' best ideas, encouraged full debate, and found ways to move the discussion forward by fostering compromise. When appropriate, he also provided his views on how the government should be constituted. Then, despite believing the Constitution was still a flawed document, Washington sought its approval by the populace, yet he did not force the issue. His facilitative approach helped gain the delegates' agreement, and his reticence in pushing for the Constitution's ratification eventually led to its acceptance by all the states.

In these various venues Washington was practicing what would later be known as "situational leadership." He adapted his leadership style to the situation. When quick decisions were required, he made them; when there was time, he sought input from his subordinates. And when a meeting of equals was dealing with the delicate and important subject of America's future government, Washington played the facilitator. In none of these roles was he perfect, but he did each well enough to achieve success of great magnitude—winning a war of independence and creating the foundations of a government that would serve as a role model to many others.

His example tells us that as modern business leaders we should not be captivated by the charismatic leader model, one in which we make all the decisions all the time and others merely follow our supposedly brilliant orders. This is especially critical in the age of the "knowledge worker," when bright, well-educated, and experienced people with good ideas want to see them implemented. We need to employ more than one style of leadership as the situation dictates, and to have the skills to do so. Probably the most difficult of these skills to learn is facilitation, as high-level leaders are often used to putting forward their decisions and having them accepted. Also, more is required to create an environment of open discussion and debate than just getting people together in a meeting room, especially if you are the leader and your subordinates are accustomed to deferring to you. But mastering this skill is crucial if you are to deploy the full range of leadership skills required in modern business.

## *Summary*

To save the Revolution, Washington displayed his **integrity** by blocking the scheme for an American monarchy or military tyranny. He not only turned down the power offered to him but took an active role in ensuring that the plot went no further.

To win the war and facilitate the formation of a better government, Washington chose to **lead in different ways**. Depending on the situation, he employed different leadership styles and tactics to achieve success.

Not incidentally, Washington also demonstrated his leadership skill at communicating with a hostile audience when he realized he was not getting through to the incipient rebels of the Newburgh Conspiracy and improvised a message that won them over.

As the first president of the fledgling United States of America, Washington would need these and many other skills. This is the story to be told in the next chapter.

# 9 ▪ Foundations of Freedom
## *A Vision for the Future*

### *The First President: Creating the Role
and Establishing the Culture*

Once the Constitution had been accepted by the people, it was time to elect the first federal government officials. Given Washington's service to the country and the trust he had among the founding fathers, there was little doubt in anyone's mind who would be the first president of the United States. And so it was that in February 1789, George Washington was unanimously chosen by the electoral college. In this new role of president, he knew that every action he took would set a precedent for his successors. This was a heavy burden in itself, but even more important, Washington, with the other members of government, was directly responsible for the early success or failure of the American experiment. Not only did the freedom of the American people rest in the balance, but the world would look to America to see if the experiment in republicanism would work.

Washington clearly recognized both of these responsibilities. On setting precedent he acknowledged, "I walk on untrodden ground. There is scarcely any part of my conduct which may not hereafter be drawn into precedent." And in his inaugural address on April 30, 1789, Washington told the country that "the preservation of the sacred fire of liberty, and the destiny of the Republican model of Government" was based on "the experiment entrusted to the hands of the American people."

From the beginning of his career Washington had a vision for what the country could become. He carried that vision into his presidency and sought to ensure a well-ordered government based on both laws and reason. He believed that through using reason and being open to various viewpoints, citizens could arrive at proper laws and policies to ensure peace, prosperity, and happiness for the country. If the citizens used this approach there would be no need for factions or parties that Washington saw as a danger to the republic.

To ensure a proper balance within the government Washington wanted to follow the Constitution carefully and use it as his compass. He did not want to encroach on the other branches, but he also expected to exercise fully the rights of the executive branch so that it retained its full powers.

Washington sought the best men available to fill the key openings in his cabinet (in fact, one precedent Washington had to set was the right of the president to select his own cabinet). He believed that men of reason and capability would produce good government. He also avoided appointing those he felt unqualified, turning down his nephew's request to be the U.S. attorney for Virginia because he knew others who were more able. He selected Thomas Jefferson as the secretary of state; as secretary of the treasury he chose his former aide Alexander Hamilton; for secretary of war he picked his old army colleague Henry Knox; and as attorney general, Edmund Randolph. Washington relied heavily on a fellow Virginian, James Madison, as an unofficial advisor. As events would prove, these men would make great contributions to laying the foundations of the federal government. However, philosophical differences between Hamilton and Jefferson would lead to formation of the factions that Washington feared.

To come to the best possible decisions on government policy, Washington followed a practice he had learned as a general—getting input from his subordinates. He met with them frequently and, keeping an open mind, sought their insights before making policy decisions.

Although it was codified in the Constitution and therefore not technically a precedent set by Washington, it was Washington's leadership during the war that led the Constitutional Convention to make the president the commander-in-chief of all the armed forces. Washington's effectiveness in carrying out the war while still working with Congress and submitting to its will persuaded the founding fathers to give this powerful role to the executive.

Washington also sought to unite the country and win its acceptance and even fondness for the new federal government. He toured the new country and personally met with the people in the states, beginning with New England in 1789 and continuing in the South in 1791. These personal encounters led the citizenry to identify the budding government with the popular figure of Washington, thus strengthening their support for it.

Beyond forming the organization of the executive, Washington also created its culture. He disdained the ostentatious methods of courts of Europe and agreed with the House of Representatives to simply be called "the president" instead of, as had been recommended, "His Most Benign Highness." He also wanted his surroundings to be well furnished yet simple. That did not mean Washington would be overly familiar with people. He maintained his studied reserve with all audiences. With these means he ensured that the office of the presidency reflected the equality of the republic yet sustained a high level of respect and deference from its citizens and foreigners.

### Foundations for Growth

Washington knew three things were critical for the new nation: freedom to expand westward to the agreed-upon boundaries of the new United States, a strong central government to make certain the union of states stayed together during the westward expansion, and avoidance of a debilitating and distracting war with the European powers that would stunt America's growth and potentially threaten its existence. All these issues were interrelated. Blocking the expansion westward were Britain, Spain, and the Indian tribes. Britain had ceded large tracts of land to the fledgling United States in the treaty ending the Revolutionary War, the most important being the Ohio River Valley. However, the British still maintained a presence in the area, using the lack of payment of American debts as an excuse. They also encouraged the Indian tribes to resist the purchase of their lands by Americans and incited them to attack American settlements in the Ohio River Valley.

Spain sought to stop the American advance toward Louisiana (a territory it had gained as a result of the war) by closing the mouth of the Mississippi to Americans and using Indians to hold back the flow of settlers. Spain also owned Florida, blocking total American ownership of the eastern seaboard.

Adding to this challenging situation, France was going through its own revolution. As France had been an ally in the war and was now (at least as some thought at the time) emulating the American experiment in republicanism, there was a great deal of support for her in the colonies. Yet France's constant conflict with Britain often caught Washington and America in the middle of those struggles. To deal with this difficult state of affairs Washington knew he needed a capable military and a financially strong government.

It was to rebuild the country's finances that Washington had brought Hamilton in as secretary of the treasury. Hamilton introduced several farsighted policies to strengthen commerce and build industry, including a proposal for a national bank. Although Hamilton's policies created concern among many (especially Jefferson, who had a vision of an agrarian rather than an industrial society), Washington supported most of his ideas and helped his proposals become policy and law. Hamilton's efforts put the U.S. government on a robust financial footing as early as 1791.

To deal with Spain, Washington sought to use diplomacy. Unsuccessful efforts by Washington's envoy William Short had achieved nothing, and some states and settlers were getting rest-less. The threat that they might attach themselves to Spain spurred Washington to send Thomas Pickney to Madrid; in 1795 Pickney negotiated a treaty that allowed Americans to use the Mississippi and the port of New Orleans for trade.

Dealing with the British and French was much more com-plex. Washington saw that trade with Britain would ensure eco-nomic growth. He also knew that Britain, not France, was in a position to threaten the United States and limit her expansion. So a conciliatory policy toward Britain held many advantages. Yet popular support for France was a powerful force, and in the conflict between the two European powers most Americans sided strongly with France. Within Washington's government there was a split on policy, with Hamilton favoring better relations with the British and Jefferson advancing a pro-French policy.

*Opening the Northwest Territory*

Washington took both a military and a diplomatic approach to open the "Northwest Territory" in the Ohio River Valley, first using the diplomatic route. Treaties with some of the Indian tribes were negotiated with the intention of purchasing land and avoid-ing fighting. However, other tribes refused to recognize the treaties and continued to attack settlements and kill the inhabi-tants. Washington, who early had hoped, perhaps naively, that the Indians would adopt European ways, eventually saw this would not be the case and authorized the army to enforce the treaties. However, initial military attempts to protect settlers met with disaster when the tribes, led by Chief Little Turtle, destroyed one sizable force under Colonel John Hardin. Washington then looked to former Revolutionary War commander Arthur St. Clair who was now the senior commander in the army. St. Clair led a second expedition into the Northwest Territory. This one too was am-bushed by Little Turtle on November 4, 1791, and the ensuing battle turned into one of the worst defeats in the army's history. As a result, Washington requested St. Clair's resignation from the army and appointed his old and trusted comrade Mad Anthony

Wayne to defeat the Indians. Wayne was appointed in 1792 and in May 1793 came to the Territory. Unlike his predecessors, Wayne took the time to train his troops hard and prepare the necessary logistics to support the next incursion. Wayne's force pushed into the Northwest Territory and in the Battle of Fallen Timbers on August 20, 1794, dealt the Indians a major blow. The Indians had hoped the British would then come to their aid, but not seeking war with the United States and seeing their Indian allies defeated, England demurred. The resulting Treaty of Greenville in 1795 secured the Ohio River Valley for the United States, and Washington achieved another major objective, one that would allow the new nation to expand farther westward.

### The Jay Treaty

Washington preferred that America stay neutral and out of the way when European powers clashed. He knew that neutrality and avoiding war would allow America the time to grow stronger. However, navigating seas troubled by France and Britain was difficult, especially when they went to war with one another in 1793. As part of the War of Independence, the United States had signed a treaty with France in 1778 in which the two nations agreed to be allies should either war with Great Britain. And it was France whose help had ensured the ultimate success of the Revolution. Yet revolutionary France was led by hotheads who were using the guillotine to eradicate their nobility. So Washington, taking the lead in foreign policy for the executive, declared America's neutrality in spring of 1793. He went further in 1794, sending John Jay, the first chief justice of the Supreme Court, to gain an agreement with Britain. The goal of the negotiations was to come to an understanding with Great Britain to avoid war, to ensure it honored the Treaty of Paris by evacuating its forts in the Northwest Territory, and to increase commerce between the two nations.

The Jay Treaty did gain Britain's agreement to evacuate the Northwest Territory but otherwise heavily favored British military and commercial interests. Thus it was received with great indignation in the United States, especially given the citizens' fervor for revolutionary France and its antipathy toward Britain. Anger toward Jay and even Washington was high, and the split between the pro-British Hamilton-led party and the pro-French Jefferson-led faction grew even wider (in 1794 Jefferson would resign as secretary of state). Passions were intense, and some citizens signaled their displeasure by either guillotining or burning John Jay in effigy (Jay himself wryly commented that he could have navigated his way through the land that year by following the beacons of his burning effigies). At times even violence took hold. Washington, who always tried to be as dispassionate as possible in his deliberations, was taken aback. He would write Hamilton, "At present the cry against the Treaty is like that against a mad dog."

Public debates and political maneuvering by the parties on both sides ensued. Despite opposition, Hamilton and his allies were able to gain enough support for the treaty to push it through the Senate for approval and Washington signed it. However, the House of Representatives, with its power of the purse, threatened to withhold the appropriations necessary to implement the agreement. To stop the treaty, its opponents in the House demanded that Washington divulge all communications (including private ones) within his administration with regard to the document. Washington rejected the request diplomatically, referring the House to the Constitution, which stated that only the executive and Senate made foreign policy. Thus Washington secured the leadership of the executive in foreign relations. Hamilton then whipped up popular support that led the representatives to vote the appropriations bills through, and the treaty was ready for implementation. In the end, the Jay Treaty proved beneficial to the United States, achieving Washington's aims of keeping the country out of war, securing the Northwest Territory, and encouraging commerce.

## The Whiskey Rebellion

During Washington's time in office he sought to strengthen the central government to hold the country together. He did this mainly by seeking to attach the citizenry's affection and the states' support by balancing the needs of the various groups. His tours of the country, his support for building a new capitol for the nation, and his reverence for the Constitution all served this purpose. However, although always ready to listen to both sides of an argument, Washington would not countenance advancing group interests or threatening the government through violence.

An excise tax put on whiskey by Congress in 1790 angered the settlers in the mountains of western Pennsylvania, who saw it as an infringement on their rights. It was also a financial hardship; they distilled their grain into whiskey because whiskey was easier to transport than grain and could be used as money or to barter. Further points of contention among these pioneers were the federal government's failure to protect them against Indian attacks and its lack of progress in opening the Mississippi to their trade. Finally, they saw the excise tax as a burden placed on them by rich easterners who knew nothing of the settlers' world and sought to take advantage of these westerners. Far from the central government, they saw it more as an enemy that taxed them than a friend that would help.

Although Washington was able to persuade legislators to reduce the impositions of the law, violent opposition to it broke out in July 1794 when a federal marshal went after several evaders of the tax. Fearing that many citizens would be jailed, the community reacted by attacking the house of the government tax collector. Fighting there left three men dead, the tax collector's house burned to the ground, and the federal marshal forced to disavow support for the tax. Committees began to spring up throughout the mountains threatening further violence and even secession from the union. Eventually twenty counties in four states would be involved.

Washington took a two-pronged approach. He sent mediators to the area to hear the settlers' grievances, offer amnesty, forgive back taxes, yet demand their profession of loyalty by September 1. At the same time Washington called up 13,000 militiamen to show the government's resolve. The rebels had a choice: submit peacefully with an agreement or continue the insurrection.

Unfortunately, Washington's olive branch was rejected, so the army had to take the field, with General Harry Lee at its head and Washington himself joining it in full uniform. Although some feel Washington overreacted to the threat, remember that this was the time of the French Revolution with all its excesses. Luckily for Washington, as the government army moved west, news of Wayne's victory at Fallen Timbers reached the area. This bolstered the government's position and also held the promise of more land and prosperity for the mountain settlers. In the end the army proceeded through the mountains and by its presence enforced the government's will. It encountered no opposition, and the Whiskey Rebellion concluded with no more spilled blood. Washington had eliminated the threat to the central government through an astute mixture of carrots and sticks, ensuring the legitimacy of the Constitution.

### Last Acts: A Proper Time to Retire

"No consideration under heaven that I can foresee shall again draw me from the walks of private life." So wrote Washington in 1796 as his second term drew to a close. He felt that he had given all he had to give to the country and wished to retire to Mount Vernon to enjoy the life of a gentleman farmer. Beyond his personal reasons to retire, Washington had professional reasons to leave office. He was concerned that as he grew older he was losing some of his faculties; he wanted to ensure that the new country could be led by someone younger and more vigorous. And while he had achieved major accomplishments during his time in office, he had also suffered many attacks on his policies due to the rise of political factions. He had even been accused again of plotting a return to monarchy. In part to rebut the latter claim but also to show that the new nation could successfully execute the democratic and peaceful transition of power, Washington felt that retiring after two terms would provide a guide to current and future generations of politicians. As such, his two terms in office set a final precedent for presidents and would remain the norm for almost a century and a half until President Franklin D. Roosevelt broke it. Eventually the nation would codify Washington's two-term precedent into the Constitution in the Twenty-second Amendment in 1951.

In preparing to leave, Washington sought to impart guidance to the citizenry of the fledgling country to increase its chances of success and long-term prosperity. In his 1796 Farewell Address, he began by giving the reasons for his retirement from the political scene and then proceeded to pass on the wisdom he had gained through the years, asking the people to view his words as "the disinterested warnings of a parting friend, who can possibly have no personal motive to bias his counsel."

The first theme Washington sounded was the importance of maintaining the Union. Focusing on the interdependencies of four regions of the country he besought his countrymen to realize the immense benefits union held: namely, a stronger defense from attack, increased commerce and resources, political stability, and avoiding wars between different regions and states. Speaking directly to the people Washington said, "Citizens, by birth or choice, of a common country, that country has a right to concentrate your affections. The name of American, which belongs to you in your national capacity, must always exalt the just pride of patriotism more than any appellation derived from local discriminations."

Washington also spoke of the importance of the Constitution, of following its principles, ensuring that no branch of government encroached on another, and avoiding reinterpretation or rash change in it. "If, in the opinion of the people, the distribution or modification of the constitutional powers be in any particular wrong, let it be corrected by an amendment in the way which the Constitution designates. But let there be no change by usurpation; for though this, in one instance, may be the instrument of good, it is the customary weapon by which free governments are destroyed."

Washington counseled the people against the formation of factions and political parties, stating that while they may "now and then answer popular ends, they are likely, in the course of time and things, to become potent engines, by which cunning, ambitious, and unprincipled men will be enabled to subvert the power of the people and to usurp for themselves the reins of government." Furthermore, the formation of parties "agitates the community with ill-founded jealousies and false alarms, kindles the animosity of one part against another, foments occasionally riot and insurrection."

Washington advised the citizens on the need for morality based on religious principles and encouraged them to be an informed citizenry so as to make the proper decisions in their self-government, stating, "Of all dispositions and habits which lead to political prosperity, religion and morality are indispensable supports.... Promote, then, as an object of primary importance, institutions for the general diffusion of knowledge.... It is essential that public opinion should be enlightened."

Ending on the subject of foreign relations and defense, Washington warned his countrymen to stay clear of entanglements in the interests and wars of other nations, not becoming attached to or the constant enemies of any nation, and to build a strong defense. By following Washington's advice that "the great rule of conduct for us in regard to foreign nations is in extending our commercial relations, to have with them as little political connection as possible," the United States would be free to set its own course.

Washington then ended the Farewell by commenting that while he was sure some errors had been committed during his time in office, they were by no means intentional, and that the major goal of his presidency had been to "endeavor to gain time to our country to settle and mature its yet recent institutions, and to progress without interruption to that degree of strength and consistency which is necessary to give it, humanly speaking, the command of its own fortunes." Indeed he had.

Washington said his good-byes at the inauguration of new president John Adams on March 4, 1797, where a tearful audience saw him wish success to the incoming government and bow in thanks for their appreciation of his service. Before leaving Philadelphia, Washington made sure that the rent on the presidential mansion was paid in full and his household servants given ample reward for their service (in some cases up to a full year's salary), and then headed home. After being received by the citizenry of various cities along his route Washington reached Mount Vernon on the afternoon of March 15. There he would be "once more seated under my own vine and fig tree" where he would "hope to spend the remainder of my days."

Washington's retirement was for the most part like his first, a cycle of hosting guests, managing his farms and business interests, and being the family patriarch. Unfortunately, retirement lasted only a short time. During his usual morning horseback inspection of the plantation on December 12, 1799, Washington was caught in a cold rainstorm. The next day he caught a fever and had a sore throat, the latter rapidly worsening. He soon had trouble breathing and treatments were of no avail, for he had what was known at the time as "quinsy," or a sore throat so bad it often proved lethal.

Washington was calm as he prepared to meet his fate. He organized his wills and made those in the room aware that he knew his time was near, at the same time apologizing for the inconvenience he was causing. Included in his last words were "I die hard, but I am not afraid to go." On December 14, Washington died.

One of the acts taken by Washington occurred after his death, through his will. In that document Washington gave direction that at his wife Martha's death all his slaves would be freed and those incapable of taking care of themselves would receive pensions. This direction Martha carried out, taking it upon herself to free them earlier.

### Creating the Culture and Laying Foundations for Growth in Business

When Washington became president he knew his actions would set precedents for future chief executives. More important, he understood that the decisions he made could either start the United States on the path to greatness or cause the grand experiment in self-government to fail. Washington's judicious actions established a powerful, effective, and yet limited role for the executive branch, helped create the tone and culture of the new government, and planted the seeds of expansion of the young nation.

A great example of a leader in business creating a culture and putting his firm on the path for growth and prosperity is Ken Iverson at Nucor. At the time Iverson joined the Nuclear Corporation of America in 1962 (the name change to Nucor came in 1972) it was a conglomerate with a checkered past. Founded in 1905 as the Reo Motor Company by R. E. Olds (founder of Oldsmobile), it was an auto manufacturer until it went bankrupt in the 1930s. Then it became a defense contractor during the war years until it folded again after World War II, after which its core business became nuclear instrumentation. At this time it was re-christened the Nuclear Corporation of America. The new name and business focus didn't change the company's luck as it continued to lose money. A new investor purchased the firm in 1960 and gave it a new strategy that was all the rage at the time—to become a conglomerate. This approach proved a failure as well, as only one division in the company was making any money in 1965. That was Vulcraft, the steel joist and girder division run by Iverson since he joined the company. Deciding to back a winner, the owner made Iverson the CEO and gave him one goal: become profitable.

Like Washington, Iverson had the right skills for the job. His educational background was technical. Born in 1925 he had earned degrees in aeronautical engineering and metallurgy. However, he also had hands-on business experience from prior jobs in development, sales, and management. With his job experience and training, Iverson had a dynamic balance of theory and practice as well as a powerful combination of technological and business skills.

Iverson also had the kind of vision about the future of the company and its people that Washington had brought to his presidency. To lead the company that would become Nucor back from the brink and set it on the path to becoming a business legend, Iverson had a leadership philosophy, a business strategy, a belief in technology, and hard-nosed business acumen. Iverson put his philosophy on business leadership this way: "I think there are probably two things that are very important to most people and certainly to hourly workers. One is what am I going to get paid and the second is, am I going to have a job tomorrow?" Iverson felt that if he could find the right workers and create an incentive system that provided them with better answers to those questions than other companies, their resulting productivity would provide a major competitive advantage. This productivity could be further multiplied by the introduction of new technologies that other companies were too entrenched to introduce. Iverson's initial strategy was to focus Nucor around the success of his Vulcraft division and jettison or shut down the money-losing divisions as soon as possible. He would also reduce costs by eliminating management layers, moving the headquarters to Charlotte, North Carolina, from Phoenix, and cutting the number of corporate headquarters positions.

In two short years Iverson had turned Nucor around. The heart of his success was his approach to people management, primarily through his incentive system. Essentially, all employees were paid bonuses tied to their productivity—from workers on the floor to department heads to the executives. If a Nucor worker produced above quota he could double his base pay and make more than his union counterpart (and since Nucor's locations were in rural areas, significantly more than other local workers). The system wasn't all upside though; those who were absent or tardy lost their right to bonuses and, if it happened frequently enough, were let go. This approach weeded out those who wouldn't perform and left the cream of the crop—motivated and productive individuals who fit in the system. Around this core incentive system Iverson added other practices. For example, there were no special perks for executives; the same set of benefits was available to all. Also, if industry demand dropped, wages might go down for all, but no one would be laid off. Perhaps more important, the people on the floor were seen as the experts and given the green light to solve their own problems and improve their productivity. The minimal layers of management meant the leadership team knew what was going on and was willing to pitch in and get their hands dirty as well. These were the keys to Iverson's and Nucor's initial success.

It was at this point that opportunity knocked and Iverson answered. Noticing that the steel Nucor was paying for consumed over half its revenues, Iverson looked for cheaper steel. Although he was already buying from European companies who offered lower prices than American producers, Iverson thought Nucor might be able to produce steel at even lower prices with his more productive people and by applying European technology. The cost advantage of the Europeans was due to the "mini-mill"— smaller mills that produced steel by melting scrap metal versus refining iron ore.

To successfully run a mini-mill Nucor would have to implement two new technologies—the electric arc furnace to melt the scrap metal and continuous casting, which formed the steel into usable shapes without cooling it. Iverson and Nucor took on the challenge, and in 1969 the company opened its first mini-mill in Darlington, South Carolina. Soon it was supplying more steel than the company could use internally and began to sell steel profitably to other firms.

Like Washington, Iverson liked to seize opportunities. He now recast Nucor's strategy around providing quality, low-cost steel and expanded wisely, building new plants to meet growing demand for Nucor's steel as sales soared. He chose rural areas where taxes were low, unions were weak, and his pay structure would attract the best workers. The result was increasing revenue and profits in an industry where other players were losing money and declaring bankruptcy.

To continue his success Iverson didn't just stop at transferring the existing European mini-mill technology; he found new technologies he could implement as well. The biggest challenge was in the 1980s when Nucor became the first company to actually implement a process that until then was theory: thin-slab casting. Nucor built the first thin-slab cast mill in Crawfordsville, Indiana. Overcoming naysayers and huge technological obstacles with hard work and ingenuity, Nucor's "bet the company" gamble paid off by allowing it to enter new markets for thin-slab sheets as a low-cost leader. This provided another jump upward in Nucor's growth curve.

Iverson retired from Nucor in 1996, and his results speak for themselves. During his thirty years at Nucor's helm revenue grew from $21 million to $3.6 billion, earnings grew from $1.3 million to $248 million (Nucor was profitable every quarter after 1966), and the stock price went from twelve cents a share to $25.50 per share. Under Dan DiMicco, Nucor's current CEO and a twenty-three-year Nucor veteran, the company has continued to prosper using Iverson's performance-based incentive system and remains a technology leader. DiMicco has tweaked the formula by expanding globally (Iverson wanted to stay domestic) and acquiring plants versus building them, but it's essentially the classic Nucor approach. The number of headquarters employees is only sixty-six, technology is still a leverage point, and employee productivity remains a competitive advantage. The names of all 11,600 employees continue to be listed on the front and back pages of the annual report. While Nucor's 2005 revenue is now $12.7 billion with earnings of $1.3 billion, DiMicco's pay is only twenty-three times that of the lowest-paid Nucor employee (the average CEO makes 400 times what a typical plant worker is paid). And the no layoff policy is still in effect. Like Washington, Iverson left a culture and approach that laid the foundation for the continued growth and success of Nucor, which it still enjoys today.

### A Proper Time to Retire in Business

When is the right time for a CEO—or for that matter, any business leader—to retire? Washington's choices in the timing of his retirement give guidance.

Washington was concerned that he was losing the full extent of his capabilities and wanted the office of the presidency to be filled by a person more youthful and in full possession of his skills and abilities. It is a sad fact of life, but aging and the potential loss of energy or capabilities, while today can be put off longer and longer, is a factor a CEO or manager needs to consider. It takes a vigorous person at the top of his or her game to lead a company or a team. When energy and interest start to fail, it may be in the best interests of all to pass the baton.

Washington also wanted to set a precedent future presidents could follow on an appropriate length of service. While few want to see a successful executive leave, sometimes a change in personnel or strategy can be good. In the example above, Ken Iverson argued against Nucor's executing an acquisition strategy and going global. However, Dan DiMicco showed that both approaches could be implemented if done wisely and in accordance with Nucor's culture (for example, Nucor will only acquire plants whose culture is similar enough to meld in with the company's work patterns, and a lot of attention is given to grafting the Nucor culture onto the acquired unit so it can quickly come up to speed).

Age and length of service are two key factors to consider. Contribution to the business and the availability of potential replacements are others. If over time the results of the CEO or manager have been declining, it's time to look for new leadership. However, it's critical to have a bench from which new leaders can be selected and a range of external connections to find talent outside the company. Another consideration is retaining talented people. While the leader may still be doing a good job, if there is no sign of when he may leave, gifted subordinates may move to other companies for advancement.

Personal considerations played a role in Washington's retirement; they should as well in business. Today, with so many opportunities to take pleasure in life after work, each of us should think about when to reward ourselves with time to enjoy other experiences.

In retiring, Washington gave guidance to future Americans in his Farewell Address. This could also be appropriate for a retiring CEO. However, once he left office Washington refrained from giving advice to his successor or commenting on policy. This is the same policy a retiring CEO should practice. Whether it's leading the government or leading a business, nothing is more disruptive and unhelpful than meddling by the past leader.

### Summary

To help the new nation survive and prosper, Washington returned to serve as the first president of the United States. As the first chief executive, Washington had the **vision** and ability to

**create the role** of president and set many precedents his successors would follow. He also was able to **establish the culture** of the executive and influenced that of the rest of the government.

Washington's policy decisions **laid the foundations of growth** for the United States and set it on the path to greatness. Whether dealing with the European powers or making domestic decisions, he looked at all points of view and made his decisions rationally based on the interests of the country. He always did his best not to allow personalities and emotions to interfere.

Washington chose his retirement with an eye to the future as well. He selected **a proper time to retire** based on his capabilities but more important, on what was best for the country. Once he left office he refused to meddle in the affairs of the new government.

In the final chapter we will review all of Washington's leadership principles and give thought to how each of us may implement them in our business lives.

# 10 ▪ Washington's Principles of Leadership

Much can be learned about leadership in general and business leadership specifically by understanding the life and career of General and then President George Washington. At a young age he worked on improving himself intellectually, morally, and physically. He developed **self-discipline, strong character, courage**, a desire to **learn**, and a bent for **innovative ideas**. Early in the Revolutionary War Washington had to develop excellent **organizational abilities** to create a new army from scratch. Throughout the war he exhibited the **persistence** to continue the fight despite numerous setbacks and mistakes. His ability to do so still astonishes today.

When war came, Washington formulated a **vision** of what the new country could become. This was the overarching guide for his leadership as general and then as president, and he never lost sight of that vision. Washington was smart enough to **develop a strategy** that maximized the strengths of the colonies while taking advantage of the political situation in Britain and the world. He knew he had to keep his army intact to keep the Revolution alive, and yet he was not afraid to **seize opportunities** for victories that would rally the populace and bring France into the war on the American side. In these battles Washington utilized **quick thinking under pressure** to avoid the destruction of his army or to achieve victory. Washington **built a winning team** of officers he could count on to give him other points of view and to carry out his orders. Using an **intelligence** network he personally devised, he used this knowledge to overcome his many other disadvantages and win battles such as the ones at Trenton and Princeton. Simultaneously, Washington developed a **personal network** with the leading men of the colonies to influence them to support his plans and the Cause. To **maintain support of the troops** and the citizenry, Washington supplied the newspapers with a steady stream of information to keep them aware of the reasons for the war and its progress. To bring the war to a successful conclusion, Washington managed the difficult alliance with France in a way that fostered cooperation and brought eventual victory.

After independence was achieved, Washington was offered a chance to overthrow the republic and install himself as king. His **integrity** led him to reject it and stop the monarchical movement in its tracks. Washington then took a key role in the development of the Constitution, **leading by facilitating** the Constitutional Convention to create a document that would provide a firm foundation for the new country yet enable flexibility for change over time.

Washington was then naturally drafted to become the first president of the United States. In that role his **wisdom** led him to set high standards that future presidents would look to for guidance and by which their terms would be measured. Washington was also able to see where the future of the country lay, and he did his best to maintain peace while securing the new nation's frontiers and maintaining domestic stability. He was above all both practical in his thinking and action oriented in his activities. His presidency, while far from perfect, set the new nation on its trajectory to greatness. Retiring after two terms to allow new people to implement new ideas and have their turn at leading the country,

Washington retired to Mount Vernon, leaving a legacy that would last for centuries.

While he made his share of mistakes, you might rightly ask, "How can I expect to live up to Washington's achievements?" Admittedly, he set the bar very high in his impact on history and his own personal behavior. You might well look at your own achievements and conduct—as good as they might be—and decide you could never consistently meet his standards. So how should Washington's life and career be used as a role model?

I think we should strive to live up to the example George Washington set in terms of his character traits and conduct. Certainly we can do better following Washington's example than those of many of today's flashier business and political leaders or sports and rock stars. We may not meet the mark every day, but if we do our utmost to follow his lead, we can become better individuals, leaders, and businesspeople. We may not choose to follow Washington's reserved personal style (although while Washington was often quite formal, he certainly enjoyed a little gambling, a good joke, and the company of the opposite sex). We need to be ourselves. But by learning his "principles of leadership" and following his example we can become a better version of ourselves.

# BIBLIOGRAPHY

Below are the books I used as resources about Washington. All were very helpful, but the ones I relied upon most include *His Excellency: George Washington* by Joseph J. Ellis, *Washington's Crossing* by David Hackett Fischer, *Washington's Secret War: The Hidden History of Valley Forge* by Thomas Fleming, *Washington: The Indispensable Man* by James Thomas Flexner, *The War for American Independence* by Samuel B. Griffith II, *George Washington—A Biography* by Washington Irving, *Victory at Yorktown: The Campaign that Won the Revolution* by Richard M. Ketchum, *George Washington's War: The Saga of the American Revolution* by Robert Leckie, and *The Glorious Cause: The American Revolution, 1763–1789* by Robert Middlekauff.

Achenbach, Joel. *The Grand Idea: George Washington's Potomac and the Race to the West.* New York: Simon and Schuster, 2004.

Billias, George Athan, ed. *George Washington's Generals and Opponents: Their Exploits and Leadership.* New York: Da Capo Press, 1994.

Boatner, Mark M. III. *Encyclopedia of the American Revolution.* Mechanicsburg, PA: Stackpole Books, 1994.

Buchanan, John. *The Road to Valley Forge: How Washington Built the Army that Won the Revolution.* Hoboken, NJ: John Wiley, 2004.

Burns, James MacGregor, and Susan Dunn. *George Washington*. New York: Henry Holt, 2004.

Chadwick, Bruce. *George Washington's War: The Forging of a Revolutionary Leader and the American Presidency*. Naperville, IL: Sourcebooks, 2004.

Ellis, Joseph J. *His Excellency: George Washington*. New York: Alfred A. Knopf, 2005.

Fischer, David Hackett. *Washington's Crossing*. New York: Oxford University Press, 2004.

Fleming, Thomas. *Washington's Secret War: The Hidden History of Valley Forge*. New York: Collins, 2005.

Flexner, James Thomas. *Washington: The Indispensable Man*. Boston: Little, Brown, 1974.

Griffith, Samuel B. II. *The War for American Independence*. Urbana: University of Illinois Press, 2002.

Irving, Washington. *George Washington—A Biography*. Edited and abridged by Charles Neider. New York: Da Capo Press, 1994.

Ketchum, Richard M. *Victory at Yorktown: The Campaign that Won the Revolution*. New York: Henry Holt, 2004.

Langguth, A. J. *Patriots: The Men Who Started the American Revolution*. New York: Simon and Schuster, 1987.

Leckie, Robert. *George Washington's War: The Saga of the American Revolution*. New York: HarperCollins, 1992.

———. *The Wars of America*. Edison, NJ: Castle Books, 1998.

McIntyre, Ruluff D. "George Washington—Master of Misinformation." *Early America Review* (Winter/Spring 2004). www.earlyamerica .com/review/2004_winter_spring/washington.htm.

Middlekauff, Robert. *The Glorious Cause: The American Revolution, 1763–1789*. New York: Oxford University Press, 1982.

PBS. *Rediscovering George Washington*. www.pbs.org/georgewashington.

Rhodehamel, John, ed. *The American Revolution: Writings from the War of Independence*. New York: Library of America, 2001.

Rose, P. K. "George Washington: The First American Intelligence Chief." www.cia.gov/library/center-for-the-study-of-intelligence/ csi-publications/books-and-monographs/the-founding-fathers-of- american-intelligence/art-1.html#george-washington-the-first.

Royster, Charles. *A Revolutionary People at War: The Continental Army and American Character, 1775–1783*. Chapel Hill: University of North Carolina Press, 1979.

Smith, Richard Norton. *Patriarch: George Washington and the New American Nation*. Boston: Houghton Mifflin, 1993.

Sword, Wiley. *President Washington's Indian War: The Struggle for the Old Northwest, 1790–1795*. Norman: University of Oklahoma Press, 1985.

Weigley, Russell F. *The American Way of War: A History of United States Military Strategy and Policy*. Bloomington: Indiana University Press, 1977.

Weintraub, Stanley. *General Washington's Christmas Farewell: A Mount Vernon Homecoming, 1783*. New York: Free Press, 2003.

Below are the primary sources used for the business examples, by chapter.

## Chapter 1

Acocella, Nick. "Baseball's Showman." *ESPN Classic*. http://espn.go.com/classic/veeckbill000816.html.

Andrescik, Rob. "Don't Have a Cow!" *New Man* (November–December 2004): 19–31.

Brodsky, Norm. "Street Smarts: The Capacity Trap II." *Inc. Magazine* (December 2003): 55–67.

Darley, J. M., and C. D. Batson. "From Jerusalem to Jericho: A Study of Situational and Dispositional Variables in Helping Behavior." *Journal of Personality and Social Psychology* 27 (1973): 100–108.

George, Philip Brandt. "George Washington: Patriot, President, Planter and Purveyor of Distilled Spirits." *American History* (February 2004): 64–73.

Hofman, Mike. "Going His Way." *Inc. Magazine* (June 2002): 128.

Lidz, Franz. "Promo Sapiens." *Sports Illustrated* (November 25, 2002): 25.

"Passion for Detail: A Conversation with Thoroughbred Trainer D. Wayne Lukas." *Harvard Business Review* (May 2004): 49–54.

## Chapter 2

Baulch, Vivian M. "Harley Earl, Father of the 'Dream' Car." *Detroit News*. http://info.detnews.com/history/story/index.cfm?id=101&category=people.

Brown, Heidi, and Justin Doebele. "Samsung's Next Act." *Forbes.com* (July 26, 2004). www.forbes.com/2004/0726/102_print.html.

Delorenzon, Matt. "Back in the Game." *Road & Track* (February 2005). www.roadandtrack.com/article/asp?print_page=y&section_id=2&article_id=1825&p.

De Mesa, Alycia. "Cadillac—Fully Loaded." *brandchannel.com* (August 2, 2004). www.brandchannel.com/print_page.asp?ar_id=191&section= profile.

Garsten, Ed. "Cadillac Revival at Crossroad." *Detroit News.com* (June 1, 2003). www.detnews.com/2003/autoinsider/0306/02/b01-179498 .htm.

Golfen, Bob. "Cadillac CTS Far from the Norm." *Azcentral.com* (February 8, 2003). www.azcentral.com/class/marketplace/cars/ 0208cadillac08.html.

Kanellos, Michael. "Samsung Leads South Korean Charge." *CNET News.com* (June 24, 2004). www.zdnet.co.uk/print?TYPE=story& AT=39158506-39020442t-20000010c.

Mieczkowski, Yanek. "Just Who Was Harley Earl?" *Culture Watch.* http://hnn.us/articles/1145.html.

Rocks, David, and Moon Ihlwan. "Samsung Design." *BusinessWeek Online* (November 29, 2004). www.businessweek.com/print/magazine/ content/04_48b3910003.htm?chan=mz&.

Rusch, Robin. "Samsung Shows Its Strength." *brandchannel.com* (July 28, 2003). www.brandchannel.com/print_page.asp?ar_id=168&sec tion=main.

Sloan, Alfred P. *My Years with General Motors.* New York: Currency, 1990.

"The Top Ten Milestones by Harley Earl." www.carofthecentury .com/top_10_milestones_by_harley_earl.htm.

## Chapter 3

Brodsky, Norm. "Learning from JetBlue." *Inc. Magazine* (March 2004): 59–60.

"Code of Ethics" of Society of Competitive Intelligence Professionals. *SCIP.org.* www.scip.org/2_code.php.

Mount, Ian. "Entrepreneurs We Love: For Creating an Airline Fit for Humans." *Inc. Magazine* (April 2004): 144.

## Chapter 4

Brewster, Mike. "Pete Rozelle: The NFL's MVP." *BusinessWeek Online* (November 24, 2004). www.businessweek.com/print/bwdaily/dn flash/nov2004/nf20041124_5773_db078.

Carey, Andrew. "Embraer: High Hopes for New Planes." *CNN. com* (April 5, 2004). www.cnn.com/2004/BUSINESS/04/05/go .embraer.boetelho/index.html.

"Is Pro Football 'the Perfect Symbol' of American Values?" *Knowledge@ Wharton* (January 26, 2005). www.knowledge.Wharton.upenn .edu/index.cfm?fa=printArticle&ID=119.

Kindred, Dave. "Most Significant Developments This Century: No. 4, Pete Rozelle Becomes NFL Commissioner." *SportingNews.com* (April 21, 1999). www.sportingnews.com/archives/sports2000/mo ments/155198-p.html.

Lynch, David J. "Comeback Kid Embraer Has Hot Jet, Fiery CEO to Match." *USA Today* (March 7, 2003). http://usatoday.com/ money/industries/manufacturing/2006-03-07-embraer-usat_x_htm.

Mitchell, Russ. "The Little Aircraft Company That Could." *CNNMoney.com* (November 14, 2005). http://money.cnn.com/magazines/ fortune/fortune_archive/2005/11/14/8360683/index.htm.

NFL History. *NFL.com.* www.nfl.com/history/chronology.

Smith, Geri. "Embraer: An Ugly Duckling Finds Its Wing." *Business Week Online* (July 31, 2006). http://www.businessweek.com/ magazine/content/06_31/b3995007.htm.

Wheatley, Jonathan, Diane Brady, and Wendy Zellner. "Brazil's Embraer Hits the Stratosphere." *BusinessWeek Online* (April 19, 2004): 32–33.

## Chapter 5

Donlon, J. P. "The Eighty-nine Billion Dollar Man." *Chief Executive Magazine* (July 1, 1996). www.highbeam.com/library/docfreeprint.asp ?docid=1G1:18555984&ctrlInfo=Roun.

Eason, Henry. "The CEO Who Refreshed Coca-Cola—Roberto Goizueta." *Nation's Business* (March 1984). www.calbears.findarticles .com/p/articles/mi_m1154/is_v72/ai_3153761/print.

Greising, David. *I'd Like the World to Buy a Coke: The Life and Leadership of Roberto Goiziuta.* New York: John Wiley, 1998.

## Chapter 6

Charan, Ram. "Conquering a Culture of Indecision." *Harvard Business Review* (January 2006): 108–117.

Gerstner, Louis V. *"Who Says Elephants Can't Dance?" Leading a Great Enterprise Through Dramatic Change.* New York: HarperCollins, 2002.

Hanft, Adam. "Smarter Hiring, the DDI Way." *Inc. Magazine* (March 2003): 92–98.

Kurtz, Rod. "Testing, Testing..." *Inc. Magazine* (June 2004): 35–37.

Levering, Robert. "The Essence of Great Workplaces." *GrowTalent.com*. http://growtalent.com/gptw/bob_levering.htm.

Lewis, Michael. *Moneyball: The Art of Winning an Unfair Game.* New York: W. W. Norton, 2003.

Rosenthall, Marc. "Trust! (but Verify)." *FastCompany.com* (April 1996). www.fastcompany.com/online/02/trustsec.html.

## Chapter 7

"Apples iTunes Users Growing Fast." *BBC News* (January 23, 2006). http://news.bbc.co.uk/1/hi/technology/4639880.stm.

Benjamin, Todd. "Carlos Ghosn: Nissan's Turnaround Artist." *CNN.com* (April 2005). http://cnn.worldnews.

Darlin, Damon. "The iPod Ecosystem." *New York Times* (February 3, 2006). www.nytimes.com/2006/02/03/technology/03ipod.html ?ex=1296622800&en=91f4e87dd848693f&ei=5088.

Kahney, Leander. "Straight Dope on the iPod's Birth." *Wired.com* (October 2006). www.wired.com/gadgets/mac/commentary/cultofmac/2006/10/71956.

Tischler, Linda. "Nissan Motor Co.: Carlos Ghosn Shifts the Once-troubled Automaker into Profit Overdrive." *FastCompany.com* (June 2002): 80. www.fastcompany.com/magazine/60/nissan.html.

Welch, David. "Grading Ghosn." *BusinessWeek* (September 25, 2006): 50–51.

## Chapter 8

Davidson, Spencer. "A Replay of the Tylenol Scare." *Time Magazine* (February 24, 1986). www.time.com/time/magazine/article/0,9171 ,960693,00.html.

"Johnson & Johnson's Tylenol Scare." http://iml.jou.ufl.edu/projects/spring01/Hogue/tylenol.html.

"The Tylenol Scare." http://iml.jou.ufl.edu/projects/Fall02/Susi/tylenol .htm.

## Chapter 9

Brockerman, Steven. "Ken Iverson: Man of Steel." *Capitalism Magazine* (May 25, 2006). www.capmag.com/article.asp?ID=4678.

Byrnes, Nanette. "The Art of Motivation." *BusinessWeek* (May 1, 2006): 57–62.

"Ken Iverson—Nucor." American National Business Hall of Fame. www.anbhf.org/laureates/keniversen.htm.

"Most Inspiring Steel Boss—Dan DiMicco." *BusinessWeek* (December 18, 2006): 62.

Rolfes, Rebecca. "The Working Man's Evangelist: There's Nothing Fancy about Dan DiMicco." *Forward Online* (January/February 2006). http://forward.msci.org/articles/0206working.cfm.

Terez, Tom. "The Soft Side of a Steel Company." *BetterWorkPlaceNow.com* (2004). www.betterworkplacenow.com/iverson.html.

# INDEX